SO-AEU-422

ETIQUETTE GUIDE TO THE
PHILIPPINES

Know the rules that make the difference!

DENNIS AND JOY POSADAS

TUTTLE PUBLISHING
Tokyo • Rutland, Vermont • Singapore

Published by Tuttle Publishing, an imprint of Periplus Editions (HK) Ltd., with editorial offices at 364 Innovation Drive, North Clarendon, Vermont 05759 U.S.A.

Copyright © 2008 by Dennis and Joy Posadas
Cover photo © George Tapan

All rights reserved. No part of this publication may be reproduced or utilized in any form or by any means, electronic or mechanical, including photocopying, recording, or by any information storage and retrieval system, without prior written permission from the publisher.

Library of Congress Cataloging-in-Publication Data
Posadas, Dennis.
  Etiquette guide to the Philippines : know the rules that make the difference! / Dennis and Joy Posadas. — 1st ed.
     p. cm.
  ISBN 978-0-8048-3954-9 (pbk.)
  1. Etiquette—Philippines. I. Posadas, Joy. II. Title.
  BJ2007.P453P67 2008
  395.09599—dc22

                                              2008018325

ISBN 978-0-8048-3954-9

Distributed by:
North America, Latin America & Europe
Tuttle Publishing
364 Innovation Drive
North Clarendon, VT 05759-9436 U.S.A.
Tel: 1 (802) 773-8930
Fax: 1 (802) 773-6993
info@tuttlepublishing.com
www.tuttlepublishing.com

Japan
Tuttle Publishing
Yaekari Building, 3rd Floor
5-4-12 Osaki, Shinagawa-ku
Tokyo 141 0032 Japan
Tel: (81) 3 5437-0171
Fax: (81) 3 5437-0755
tuttle-sales@gol.com

Asia Pacific
Berkeley Books Pte. Ltd.
61 Tai Seng Avenue #02-12
Singapore 534167
Tel: (65) 6280-1330
Fax: (65) 6280-6290
inquiries@periplus.com.sg
www.periplus.com

First edition
11 10 09 08   6 5 4 3 2 1

Printed in Singapore

TUTTLE PUBLISHING® is a registered trademark of Tuttle Publishing, a division of Periplus Editions (HK) Ltd.

Contents

Preface

The Philippines is a group of 7,107 islands in the western Pacific Ocean. Known affectionately as the Pearl of the Orient, it is the only predominantly Roman Catholic country in Asia. Its people are known as Filipinos and things relating to the country are called Filipino or Philippine, such as Filipino food or Philippine culture. Historically colonized by Spain and the United States, the Philippines is now home to a modern Filipino culture that blends these foreign influences with its own traditional and religious practices and beliefs. Although largely rural with an agriculture-based economy, the Philippines is also home to thriving cosmopolitan metropolises such as Manila, its capital, and Cebu.

More and more Westerners visit the Philippines each year for both business and pleasure. These Westerners will find that knowledge of and insight into the local customs and traditions will pay off with more fruitful business relationships, better and longer lasting friendships, and a more enjoyable trip. Filipinos are generally traditional in their mindset, adopting a long-established set of norms, customs, beliefs, and values unique to the Philippines. Although Westerners may find the Filipino way of life to be exotic, the Philippines is actually considered the most westernized Asian country, due mainly to the influence of the United States.

It is our hope that this book will help visitors understand what to expect from the Philippines and from Filipinos. We hope that an enhanced knowledge of etiquette practices in the Philippines will truly enlighten and inspire our foreign visitors to discover the vibrant spirit behind the smiling and welcoming people who inhabit this warm destination, a place that is truly full of life.

As we Filipinos love to say when we welcome a visitor from foreign shores—*Mabuhay!* (Long Live!)

Dennis and Joy Posadas

Notes on the Language and Its Pronunciation

The Filipino Language

Filipino is the official national language of the Philippines, as stated in the country's 1987 constitution. However, there is actually some debate among intellectual circles about what really constitutes the national language of the Philippines. No single language is spoken consistently throughout the nation: People from Manila use Filipino in everyday conversation. In Cebu and other cities, residents are more comfortable speaking in languages such as Cebuano or English. And those who live in the far-flung provinces may use a local language—or even English.

As of 2000, Filipino was spoken by almost 30 percent of the population and today it is the most widely understood language in all regions of the Philippines. Basically adapted from the language used in the Tagalog region of the Philippines, Filipino is sometimes referred to as Tagalog (although Tagalog itself differs in that it is often used in literary endeavors, and includes words not commonly used by the mainstream population).

The Filipino language is still evolving today, thanks to academicians, the government, and the common people—as well as globalization. A prominent example of this evolution is the expansion of the old twenty-letter Tagalog alphabet into the new twenty-eight-letter Filipino alphabet.

Pronunciation of Filipino Words

The following are some notes on pronunciation pertaining to Filipino. Keep in mind that in practice, the accent marks shown here are not necessarily used in writing. Hence, the beginner may not easily get the proper intonation. This is why speakers new to the language tend to get funny reactions from Filipinos. Practice in conversation with a teacher or a local is recommended.

The vowels in Filipino are as follows:

a sounds like u in c**u**p
e sounds like e in r**e**d
i sounds like i in sard**i**ne
o sounds like o in gl**o**ve
u sounds like oo in r**oo**m

The consonants in Filipino are:

b   sounds like bu in **bu**t
k   sounds like cu in **cu**t
d   sounds like da in **d**art
g   sounds like ga in **ga**p
h   sounds like huh in **hu**h
l   sounds like lu in **lu**ll
m   sounds like ma in **ma**ma
n   sounds like nu in **nu**t
nga sounds like ng in thi**ng** with a at the end
         (no exact translation)
p   sounds like pa in **pa**pa
r   sounds like ru in **ru**t
s   sounds like su in **su**m

t sounds like tu in **tu**ck
w sounds like wha in **wha**t
y sounds like yu in **yu**k

The additional eight letters are the Spanish ñ (pronounced as *enye*) and the English c, f, j, q, v, x, and z, which are pronounced exactly as they are in English.

There are six categories of Filipino words, although only five are commonly used.

Malumay (**slower**) words do not have accent marks and the stress is on the second to the last syllable (even if there are only two syllables). Here are some common examples of this type of word:

mayaman (**rich**)
materyales (**materials**)
labada (**laundry**)
bakante (**vacant**)
demanda (**demand**)
basa (read)

Malumì (**slower**) words also stress the second to the last syllable. However, the last syllable has a glottal catch, or an abrupt pause. *Malumì* words always end with a vowel with a grave accent mark (`). Some common *malumì* words are:

bihasà (**expert**)
bagà (**lung**)
kabanatà (**chapter**)
luhà (**tear**)
pitakà (**purse**)

Mabilís (quick) words stress the final syllable and are written with an acute accent mark (´). These words are spoken quickly. Some common *mabilís* words are:

damít (clothing)
lindól (earthquake)
langgám (ant)
maís (corn)
gamót (medicine)

Maragsâ (quick) words are spoken quickly, like *mabilís* words. However, they are similar to *malumì* words in that the last syllable also has a glottal catch. *Maragsâ* words end with a vowel with a circumflex mark (^). Common *maragsâ* words include:

Kanô (American)
dagâ (rat)
dukhâ (poor)
gawâ (work)
hiyâ (shame)

Mariín words contain three or more syllables. Each of the four types above can also be *mariín* words, if they include two stressed syllables. Thus, there can be *malumay*, *malumì*, *mabilís* and *maragsâ* words with additional *mariín* accent stress. *Mariín* words can include one or two accent marks and stressed syllables. Some common *mariín* words are:

pámahalaán (government)
káwanggawâ (charity)
magkáisá (unite)

mámamayán (**citizen**)
mámayâ (**later**)

The name for each type of word is itself an example of the stress pattern—except for the *mariín* type.

CHAPTER 1

The Origins of Filipino Etiquette

Before the advent of colonization in their homeland during the sixteenth century, Filipinos were already trading with neighboring nations, including China, Malaysia, Indonesia, and the Indochinese states of Annam and Tonkin. Foreign influence became especially important in the Philippines in the fourteenth century, when Muslim missionaries arrived on the southern island of Mindanao and converted the natives there. In 1521, Portuguese explorer Ferdinand Magellan arrived in the Philippines after crossing the Pacific in search of spices on behalf of the nation of Spain. He was killed on Mactan Island in Cebu, but his arrival signaled the beginning of a period of Spanish colonization that did not end until more than three hundred years later.

Prior to these foreign influences, Filipinos worshipped native divinities like *Bathala*, the supreme god, or elements in nature such as trees and mountains. These traditions gave rise to many practices, including the use of amulets that were meant to be both good luck charms and talismans for protection against harm.

Spanish rule of the Philippines heavily influenced local thinking and behavior. The Roman Catholic religion, one of

Spain's landmark contributions to the nation, has largely shaped Filipino culture. However, a number of pre-colonial beliefs and traditions persist alongside Catholic traditions, especially in rural areas.

During the period of Spanish colonization, Filipinos were essentially subservient to their Spanish leaders. Society was delineated into classes, each of which had different rights and privileges. The Spanish colonizers, referred to as *peninsulares*, made up the ruling class. Beneath them were *insulares,* or Spaniards born in the Philippines. Then came the *illustrados,* or the more affluent and educated Filipinos. The *indios* made up the general Filipino population and were given the fewest privileges. To some extent, class discrimination (even if frowned upon) still exists today.

After hostilities flared up from the Spanish-American War, the American Navy under the command of Commodore George Dewey sailed into Manila Bay in 1898 and demolished the Spanish fleet there. Purchasing the Philippines from Spain for $20 million, the United States began a policy of "benevolent assimilation"—which was essentially an attempt to remake the Philippines in the image of America. This lasted until the Commonwealth government took over in 1935 and full independence was granted by the United States in 1946 after World War II.

The legacy of colonization has had a lasting impact on Filipinos and their culture. New visitors to the country often discover that stereotypically shy Filipinos rarely voice their opinions. Filipinos can also be accommodating to the point of seemingly giving preference to foreigners and their ways. For example, Filipinos may go out of their way to entertain visiting guests, particularly ones from the West. This almost subconscious deference toward foreigners and partiality toward foreign things is called "colonial mentality."

As a result of its two Western occupations, even the population of the Philippines changed. Intermarriages between Filipinos and foreigners resulted in multiracial offspring known as *mestizos* (if male) or *mestizas* (if female). These terms are not derogatory, and are in fact considered to be positive attributes (possibly undeservedly). Today many Filipinos are a mixture of Malay, Spanish, American, Chinese, and other heritages.

The era of American colonization resulted in a strong and deep friendship that has lasted to this day. American influence in the Philippines has also remained strong because of the migration of many Filipinos to the United States. Visiting foreigners are often amazed how familiar most Filipinos are with American culture. American brands such as Colgate, Ponds, Ivory, Ford, and Coke are just as familiar here as they are in the United States. American cultural touchstones such as Bing Crosby's "White Christmas" are perennially popular, even though many residents of this tropical country have never seen snow. This familiarity with American culture is partially the cause of the proliferation of the country's call-center industry in recent years, because it allows Filipinos to communicate easily with American callers.

One of America's most important contributions to the Philippines is the system of public education fostered by American teachers nicknamed the Thomasites in honor of the ship they arrived on in 1901—the USS Thomas. The strong public school system helped generations of Filipinos to pursue secular education up to college level. Many Filipino parents today still consider a good education to be the ultimate gift they can give their children.

Many foreigners associate the Philippines with the People Power Revolution of 1986, which ended the twenty-one-year reign of Ferdinand Marcos. Elected in 1965, Marcos ruled the country under martial law starting in 1972 and kept the media and the opposition parties in check until his removal from office in 1986. With the return of civil liberties after the "bloodless" revolution that deposed Marcos, the press resumed its position as one of the liveliest in Asia. People are generally glad that Marcos is no longer in power, but the influence of Marcos and his wife, Imelda, can still be seen in Filipino culture.

Today the Philippines has a presidential form of government, with a legislative branch made up of two bodies—the Senate and the House of Representatives, which are patterned after those of the United States. Its judicial system is also headed by a chief justice presiding over a Supreme Court.

There are many college graduates in the Philippines, but due to a lack of available opportunities they do not necessarily work in fields that require such high levels of education. For example, a foreign employer in Singapore or Hong Kong—where many Filipinos work—may find a college graduate willing to work as a domestic helper for the right price, even if the same person would not be willing to take that position in the Philippines, where wages and standards of living are often much lower. Given a choice between a prestigious but low-paying job in their homeland and a high-paying service job abroad, some Filipinos would opt for the latter. This is partially because Filipinos often support both their immediate and extended families, and high paying jobs are scarce in the Philippines.

There is also a wide quality gap among colleges in the country. Local graduates from less prestigious educational institutions are often faced with the decision to look for work abroad or accept a lower salary at home, but graduates coming from well-known universities are likely to be recruited by multinational corporations even before they step out of school.

The distribution of wealth in the Philippines is grossly uneven, with only a few families controlling most of the wealth and employing a small but growing middle class. This great economic disparity means that many Filipinos are accustomed to living a hard life. Nonetheless, the happy dispositions they usually maintain despite such hardships continue to amaze foreigners. Many Filipinos easily adjust to various situations or different cultures. It is the boat of faith that keeps the Filipino afloat in times of prolonged uncertainty and upheaval. In spite of difficulties, the Filipino can still manage to flash a smile.

The happiness of most Filipinos is also rooted in the way they strongly identify with their kin, whether they are actual blood relatives or merely affiliated with their family through participation in social ceremonies such as baptisms and weddings. While individual achievement gives most Filipinos happiness, the successes of their relatives also give them a sense of being part of the victory. The opposite is also true; when family and kin are grieving, Filipinos empathize with their suffering.

CHAPTER 2

Socioeconomic Classes

In the Philippines, there is a wide gap between the rich and the poor. In economist Bernardo Villegas' 2001 book *The Philippine Advantage*, he writes that the richest 20 percent of Filipinos are responsible for 44 to 54 percent of the total consumption of goods and services in the country, while the poorest 20 percent are responsible for only 4 to 8 percent of the total consumption. As of 2006, almost 33 percent of the population was poor, according to government statistics. As such, your etiquette may need to be tailored to fit the economic class of the individuals you are dealing with.

You can expect to be entertained in the finest and most sophisticated places in the country if you are spending time with affluent Filipinos. Many members of affluent Filipino families have had the privilege of receiving higher education, sometimes even abroad. You may discover that they are up to date on various international trends and familiar with Western ways.

But life for many Filipinos is very different from how this wealthy, privileged few live. If you are spending time with members of the less privileged classes, you probably won't be taken to fancy restaurants or nightlife hotspots. Daily wages are often low, so this sort of entertainment is out of reach for many Filipino workers. Instead, you will most likely be invited to visit their homes or taken around the city for sightseeing.

The primary interaction many foreigners living in the Philippines have with those in the poorer segments of society are with the household help that they employ. There are normally three types: the driver, the maid, and the nanny or _yaya_. Some of these employees report for work in the morning and go home to their own residence at night, but others live in the home of their employer. If you intend to have your household help stay with you, they should normally be provided a separate bedroom and bathroom for their own privacy. There should be separate male and female quarters. Typically, they are entitled to one day off a week, and their work should be limited to ten hours a day at the most. You should also remember that they are probably sending their salaries (or at least part of them) to their families in the provinces.

Be attuned to the personalities and skills of the people you employ. Try to see what kind of work each employee excels at and is most comfortable with. Depending on personality, it may be that your maid should really be your nanny, or your nanny should be your maid. A change of roles may do wonders for their work attitude.

One unfortunate result of the high poverty level in the Philippines is the presence of beggars and street children. When faced with street children, it is tempting to give them money. Keep in mind that syndicates (sometimes including the children's parents) have been known to use them for their own gain, so that the money actually goes to the syndicate and not to the child. If you want to give something, give food instead of money. Another alternative would be making donations to an institution that takes care of street children.

CHAPTER 3

The Filipino Family

Family ties are an incredibly important part of life in the Philippines. Filipinos have a strong sense of kinship with and belonging to their extended families, with whom they often have close, loving, and respectful relationships. Many adult Filipinos have parents or married children living with them in the same community or compound, and sometimes even in the same house.

Living with one's in-laws is also a common practice, either to save money or care for an elderly relative. Rather than living in a nursing home, most senior citizens in the Philippines live with one of their children. Although many young couples are coming to feel it is important to have a home of their own immediately after their wedding, they do not abandon their parents because Philippine custom still dictates that children take care of their parents in their old age.

In the Philippines, women are central to family life. Mothers are often referred to as *ilaw ng tahanan*, or "light of the home." In a traditional Filipino home, the father is the head of the family and breadwinner while the mother attends to household matters, including the finances. It is not uncommon to find Filipino men handing their salaries to their wives as a sign of love and support. Their wives are then tasked with budgeting the family income. Naturally, the one who carries the purse has much say in the way funds are allocated and how things are done. Today more women are working outside the home and occupying higher positions in the workforce, allowing them to earn their own money and in some cases even support their husbands. In response, power in the Philippines has begun to shift convincingly toward matriarchy. According to some sociologists, this matriarchal tendency is rooted in the Philippines' pre-colonial social order. It is evidenced in the expression "He is under the *saya*," literally translated as "under the woman's skirt."

Nonetheless, Philippine laws do not necessarily provide equal rights to men and women. Legislature often reflects the values common when it was enacted, and many Philippine laws were crafted decades ago and may not support equal rights. In practice, however, Filipino women enjoy equal rights with men and have long held leadership positions in business, politics, and academics. The Philippines has even had two female presidents.

Although many Filipino women subtly rule on the home front, the primary difference between the Filipino woman and her Western counterpart is that she is not a staunch feminist (although there are a few organized feminist groups in the country and in Congress). Many (if not most) women embrace traditional values and place much importance in family and home matters. Careers are usually shaped as a secondary consideration, many times out of financial necessity.

In spite of the apparent emancipation of women in the Philippines, most women actually behave submissively in personal and romantic relationships. This means that they accord respect and authority to the man of the house. The husband is often treated like a king, even if he sometimes fails to take full economic responsibility for the household. Many people believe that it is actually this attitude that endears the woman of the house to her husband and guarantees his utmost loyalty and support for his queen.

While the scenario of a husband as breadwinner and wife as manager of the home is still generally perceived to be the ideal, economic struggles have left many families unable to maintain this traditional family structure. Other families have moved away from it in response to Western influence.

In a large segment of the population one spouse will even go abroad for several years as an Overseas Foreign Worker (OFW), leaving the other spouse to take care of the family. The abundance of household helpers and extended family members available to provide childcare has allowed this to happen, even though it is not necessarily in the best interest of the children involved. Even when they live overseas, however, Filipinos still feel closely connected with their homes and families. Foreigners may be surprised by this strong connection and marvel at the number of relatives Filipinos send money to.

The importance of family ties may sometimes undermine national unity—loyalty to one's kin is often put before the needs of strangers or one's country. When the Philippines went to war against foreign powers during World War II, the nation as a whole was united. But in times of peace, national unity and equality for all become difficult to achieve—even if many Filipinos realize their value—because of the conflicting demands of loyalty to one's family, organization, or home province.

Many Filipinos tend to gravitate toward their province mates, particularly when they are abroad. Ilocanos from the north, Pampanguenos from Central Luzon, Negrenses from the Visayas, and Davaoenos from Mindanao are just some of the regional groupings that Filipinos may belong to. Some stereotypical character traits are associated with these groupings. For example, the Ilocanos are believed to be extremely thrifty while the Negrenses are believed to be very romantic.

CHAPTER 4

The Role of Religion

Some Filipinos are Protestants or members of other Christian denominations. Others belong to religious organizations such as Iglesia ni Cristo (literally translated as "Church of Christ"). Some practice Islam and a sprinkling of other faiths. However, the predominant religion in the Philippines is Roman Catholicism. Also intertwined with some of these religions are pre-colonial beliefs and traditions.

Various religions can generally coexist in harmony in the Philippines, even when a few conflicts flare up and are subsequently highlighted in the international media. The southern island of Mindanao is a promising example of how interfaith relations can work: Although once rocked by Christian-Muslim wars, particularly in the 1970s, Christians and Muslims in Mindanao now usually get along and try to work out their differences peacefully.

Whatever faith they belong to, religiosity is second nature to most Filipinos. In almost every Catholic home you will find a copy of the Bible and images of the Last Supper, the cross, and saints or other religious figures.

Most Filipinos believe in and feel a close sense of kinship with a god figure, but they may express it in different ways.

For Catholics, it is usually shown by attending Sunday mass or participating in various Catholic rites and festivals. There is also a tendency, especially in the provinces, to practice folk religion in addition to Catholicism. One example of this that is a constant source of fascination for foreigners is an annual event that takes place in the provinces during Holy Week—the week before Easter, which includes the Catholic religious holidays of Palm Sunday, Maundy Thursday (Holy Thursday), and Good Friday—that features actual crucifixions with real crosses and nails. The Catholic Church does not sanction this extreme practice, but it still exists as part of the folk religion of the Philippines. The crucifixion is usually carried out as a *panata*—a promise—made in order to earn blessings from the Almighty or as an expression of thanks for blessings received.

More traditional Catholic rites are also important to many Filipinos, including baptism and marriage. The importance of these rites helps explain why Filipinos usually go to great lengths to celebrate them.

As in other countries, this sometimes gets out of hand and these celebrations become less focused on spiritual meaningfulness than on going all-out to keep up appearances. For example, parents may delay a child's baptism for the simple reason that they don't have enough money to host a christening party, an event that necessitates preparing a multitude of dishes for relatives, friends, and guests.

Weddings are celebrated storybook-style and can also be quite costly. As a wedding is a once-in-a-lifetime event, money (or the lack of it) is not the main consideration for most couples. There is also a *pamahiin,* or superstition, among older people that in each family only one wedding can be held per year. This superstition probably originated with valid, practical concerns because hosting a wedding can be quite challenging to the pocket. So if your fiancée's sibling has already gotten married this year, you will have to wait until next year to get married. Engagements are sometimes postponed to accommodate this sequence.

There are no divorce or abortion laws in the Philippines. The government would face difficultly in passing such laws, as this is a predominantly Roman Catholic country where these things are not only major political issues but also moral ones. There is an organization known as the Catholic Bishops' Conference in the Philippines (CBCP) that usually gives insight or recommendations on moral issues that affect the country and many faithful Catholic Filipinos take its advice seriously.

CHAPTER 5

The Filipino Mindset

Filipinos are very hospitable. If you are being hosted by a Filipino or make Filipino friends during your stay, expect to be taken out to dinner and to be shown some sights if time permits. And unlike in the United States, where business visitors are normally left to their own devices during weekends and after working hours, it is not uncommon for Filipino contacts to make plans to spend time with foreigners outside of office hours. If you are planning to visit particular tourist attractions or go shopping, inform your hosts; they may actually go out of their way to take you there or to some other place you may enjoy.

The Filipino's hospitality makes this island nation a haven for visitors. Filipinos value close, personal relationships more than formal acquaintances and rarely hesitate to invite friends and even strangers into their homes, particularly during important religious events such as fiesta celebrations.

Filipino society is group oriented, and people in the Philippines are not individualists. Before they fulfill their own needs, Filipinos fulfill their duties to their families and the organizations to which they belong, such as their church. A good example of this orientation toward the greater good is the way many Filipinos who work overseas send money to their loved ones back home.

Other important concepts in Philippine society are best expressed using the Filipino language.

Hiya can refer to many things, depending on the situation. A negative understanding of it might be "shame" or "shyness." In a positive light, it can also mean "politeness" and "having a desire to behave properly." It can also indicate "hesitation" or "doubt," which can be either positive or negative, depending on the situation at hand. For example, an employee who is shy in speaking up may actually hold the solution to your problems at work. Encourage your employees to speak during staff meetings, or better still, invite them to one-on-one meetings.

Utang na loob refers to the tendency of Filipinos to remember favors or acts of kindness and feel beholden to the person who granted them. In some instances this is a positive trait, but in others it can be improper. An improper facet of *utang na loob* would be shown if a candidate in an election got funding from certain special interest groups, or even shady elements of society, and felt obligated to honor their wishes while in office. *Utang na loob* is good when it leads people to repay favors for the good of society, not for some personal or selfish motive.

Delicadeza means "a sense of honor." In public life, individuals with *delicadeza* would be prepared to resign their positions and suffer the consequences of their actions if they did something wrong. Another facet of *delicadeza* is avoiding situations that could compromise one's integrity in the first place. It is not as extreme as the Japanese practice of committing ritual suicide, or *seppuku*, but the manner of taking responsibility for one's actions is quite similar.

The word *Awa* means "a sense of pity or compassion." Although often a positive thing, *awa* may also allow emotions to cloud one's objective decision-making abilities. Because they feel compassion for the accused, people reading about criminal trials in the news may make comments like "He is too young to go to jail. I don't think he is guilty," before fully weighing the facts involved.

Bahala na is another cultural characteristic that has both negative and positive aspects. It can mean a lot of things: "I don't know how I'll do it, but I'll take care of it." "Whatever fate brings." "I'll wing it." Negatively, it implies that the person saying it has no idea or plan about how to handle an issue, but will try to figure out how to do so. The positive connotation is a "can-do" attitude; even when someone has no idea how to proceed, he or she is still willing to work until a solution is found. If you are a process-oriented manager and your employee says *"bahala na,"* then chances are you will not be pleased with his or her approach to the job. In this case, you may want to coach your employee by sharing some suggestions about how he or she could go about solving the problem or delivering the expected results.

Bayanihan is the community coming together as a team to help out an individual. Its closest English equivalent is probably "teamwork." An old and popular example of *bayanihan* is a group of villagers working together to help fellow villagers transport their home to another location by carrying it. In a work context, *bayanihan* would indicate that your employees agree to work together to achieve a common goal.

CHAPTER 6

Praise

Some Filipinos can be shy about acknowledging praise. They do not normally want to attract attention to themselves and would rather refrain from boasting.

Given the Philippines' history of subservience to two colonizing nations, it is not surprising that many Filipinos have adopted a meek and humble attitude with regard to receiving praise. During the Spanish and American periods Filipinos didn't have much say in anything, even their own lives. More often than not they were subject to the good or bad deeds of their colonizers and the typical expectation was that of compliance.

In the workplace, do not be surprised if Filipinos choose to keep their accomplishments to themselves or stay low key about them. A person who remains patient, humble, and good amid trials as well as successes is described as *uliran*, or "exemplary." For example, *ulirang ina* ("exemplary [or model] mom") is often used to describe a woman who has suffered and loved greatly. On the flip side, the idea of bragging about one's achievements is taboo and anyone who does so is bound to be branded as *mayabang*, or boastful.

While it may seem that Filipinos do not care for praise, in reality they tend to perform better when positive aspects of their work are highlighted. Encouragement in the form of recognition for a job well done will motivate them to work even harder.

CHAPTER 7

Saving Face

A nother aspect of *hiya* or "shame"—a word that was discussed in a previous chapter—is saving face, or avoiding shame and embarrassment caused by oneself or by another individual. Saving face is an important aspect in social relations because the desire to save face keeps Filipinos from engaging in conflict. Contrary to what may be portrayed in the media, Filipinos do not normally engage in open confrontation or debate.

Because of this concern for appearances and what others think of them, criticism may not be taken well, especially if done publicly. One generalization that probably applies to most Filipinos is the advice to "praise in public, but scold in private."

To avoid causing your employees to lose face, criticism is best dished out in a positive or encouraging manner. Most Filipinos can accept criticism given in a non-threatening and friendly manner. More than anything, Filipinos value good friendships, which includes being sensitive to receiving criticisms. Because Filipinos are non-confrontational in nature, it is important to set the right tone when giving criticism and be in an environment that is conducive to amicable discussion. In performance evaluations, it is also a good idea to explain the criteria used in making the evaluation.

What is seen as an insult might end up in a duel of words—or even something more serious, if tempers flare up. Unlike many Westerners, who may blow up but just move on after letting off steam, some Filipinos let their anger stay bottled up inside. This repression of anger is known as *pagtanim ng galit,* or literally "planting anger." It can be compounded when one is criticized publicly. So, be a bit careful about issuing criticism, especially in public areas.

This tendency of some Filipinos to repress anger is generally something to watch out for. Fortunately, "going postal" or engaging in acts of violence against others in a public setting is still a Western phenomenon. By contrast, Filipinos may actually be keeping score of the perceived hurts they have endured even after it seems their anger has subsided. You may encounter a problem with this with some employees. Make sure they understand that you are simply doing a job, and there is nothing personal in your comments.

According to Filipino anthropologist F. Landa Jocano, Filipinos consider their work an extension of themselves. If you are giving negative feedback to a Filipino subordinate, try to limit your criticism to the work and not the person, especially if it is the first time that the problem has come up.

One strategy that may be effective for expatriate managers is scheduling regular one-on-one meetings with subordinates. This allows their employees to express any doubts or hesitations they may have—as well as any complaints—all without the risk of publicly losing face. To keep employees from feeling micromanaged, such meetings shouldn't be scheduled too frequently. They should be held just often enough for your employees to realize that you are interested in what they are doing. Regular discussions with your subordinates, especially if they feel they can speak their minds without negative repercussion, will lead to a good relationship.

Another aspect of saving face is that Filipinos do not like to be rejected or turned down. This is why they often avoid stating things directly, preferring to "beat around the bush." If your household helper asks for a day off, for example, she may end up stating a serious reason rather than the real cause of her request. Usually, this is due to fear of being turned down. Bear in mind that many bosses have actually overextended the work schedules of household helpers. If an *amo*, or "boss," has been strict or negligent in giving leave, employees naturally turn to other means in order to get out of the house. Managing household helpers follows a different set of rules than managing professionals. Those with lesser educational attainment or underprivileged upbringings have more of a tendency to be guided by emotions rather than logic. They often resort to hints or suggestions, which you will need to interpret.

CHAPTER 8

Having Patience
and Apologizing

Pasencia is a Spanish word that means "patience." The same word with a different spelling, *pasensiya*, has been adapted in Philippine culture to not only mean patience, but also to act as a way to ask for forgiveness. *Pasensiya ka na*, translated as "please have patience," is a common expression used when seeking an aggrieved person's patience or forgiveness.

It is not by chance that this apology is used often. Filipinos tend to be quite forgiving and may easily excuse the faults of others, so admitting fault doesn't have as many negative repercussions in the Philippines as it might elsewhere. What's more, Filipinos are generally very patient, what with all the inconsistencies and inefficiencies that they must put up with daily in both their personal and professional lives.

Historically, this patient character has made Filipinos adaptable to change and allowed them to survive many hard times. Ironically, though, it is also this patience that sometimes keeps Filipinos from experiencing worthwhile change. Many Filipinos suffered for twenty-one years under the dictatorial regime of Ferdinand Marcos before rising up in a bloodless revolt in 1986. And today many people seem to have already forgotten the atrocities of this regime and have come to forgive the Marcoses and their allies.

Many people believe that the positive effects of Filipino patience outweigh the negative ones, because their forgiving attitudes have allowed Filipinos to smile even in the face of adversity.

This patience is not limitless, of course. In particular, Filipinos can be quite sensitive to discrimination or verbal abuse. Although a tendency toward patience and the concerns of *hiya*, or saving face, may keep Filipinos from openly expressing their thoughts and emotions, repressed feelings can cause them to lose their tempers and explode—especially in cases of constant or repeated abuse. Ordinarily, though, it would take much to cause this kind of outburst.

And in spite of this patience, what seems like a logical act or statement to foreigners may offend some Filipinos. For example, on many American late-night talk shows institutions and prominent personalities are fodder for jokes and sarcastic remarks. But Filipinos are more sensitive than Westerners and would ask for a formal apology for what would be accepted as nothing more than a joke in other countries. It is often a good idea to avoid sarcastic remarks or jokes, as the humor in these seemingly inoffensive statements may not translate well.

Apologizing for any misunderstandings is also a respectful thing to do. If you need to apologize, take note that Filipinos communicate both verbally and nonverbally. Filipinos also tend to be quite sensitive to the emotions of others and can sense if someone making an apology is being insincere. It is important to be sincere: If your words do not match your actions, body language, and expressions, then your apology probably won't be accepted.

Doble cara, a Spanish term that means "double-faced," was adopted by Filipinos to describe someone who is insincere and appears to be a good person but is actually a bad character.

Another way Filipinos might describe "fake" people is to use the English word *plastic.*

The Western way of apologizing by simply saying "I'm sorry" is acceptable to most Filipinos. However, making apologies is considered a private matter in the Philippines. Try to find an appropriate place where you and the other person can talk privately or at least be at ease. In some situations where the deemed offense was made publicly, a public apology may be proper. Try to calm yourself before the meeting and ensure that you have some time to think about the issue. To avoid emotional confrontations, try to ascertain if the other party is also ready to talk. Some people might choose to express their apology in writing, which is also acceptable if the situation so warrants.

CHAPTER 9

Appreciation

The best way of showing appreciation is usually through a compliment. (Flattery or physical contact may make some Filipinos uncomfortable.) As with apologies, sincerity is an important aspect of offering appreciation. Otherwise, this appreciation may be called *bola*, literally "ball," a term used to describe an insincere comment. *Mambobola* or *bolero* refers to the person giving insincere compliments. Filipinos do not trust *boleros*.

Genuine appreciation can be expressed in different ways. For personal situations, notes, cards, flowers, or sweets are common expressions of gratitude. Filipinos are quite easy to please and it doesn't take much to touch their hearts. Just keep in mind that if a man gives a woman flowers (especially red roses), it is usually interpreted in a romantic way (unless of course she is his mother or grandmother, or if he is gay).

Valentine's Day is a big event for Filipinos and an ideal time to express love and appreciation. It is one of the busiest days of the year, and gifts are exchanged by lovers as well as close friends and relatives. Many restaurants and establishments prepare specially for this big day, and Manila is usually overwhelmed with traffic. Women expect to be courted with flowers, chocolates, and a special dinner date. Children give their parents cards and notes of appreciation, while friends may exchange small gifts.

In the workplace, praise for a job well done is always appreciated. Tokens of appreciation are also welcome, including gifts during the Christmas season or when you return from traveling. Gifts brought back from trips are known as *pasalubong*. *Pasalubong* are usually small gifts, such as food items like chocolate bars or local delicacies from the place you visited. Occasionally, a manager may also decide to treat his staff to lunch for their hard work. It is also common for employers to plan an annual outing for either the entire company or its individual departments. This is a chance to recharge and get to know each other better by going to an out-of-town location. Outings like this also provide an opportunity for companies to show appreciation to their managers and staff. In certain companies, loyalty is also given recognition: A staff member who has been employed for five or ten years is sometimes given a memorable gift or a cash bonus.

Companies also purchase gifts as corporate giveaways for their loyal customers as a way of cementing their professional relationship.

CHAPTER 10

The Language of Etiquette

The way you speak to people is an important part of Philippine etiquette. Most Filipino youth, especially in the rural areas, still use the polite words *po* and *opo* when speaking to their elders. *Opo* is a standalone term that means a respectful *yes*, while *po*, when appended to a response or statement, is much like addressing the other person as *sir* or *ma'am*. For example, instead of simply saying *"Ano?"* ("What?"), a young person speaking to an elderly person will say *"Ano po?"* Instead of saying *"Oo"* ("Yes"), young people will answer older individuals by saying *"Opo."* These words are used when the age difference involved is significant, such as in conversation between a child and an adult or a young adult and a senior citizen. *Po* and *opo* may also be used when speaking to someone in authority, such as a priest, police officer, teacher, or mayor.

Although Filipinos are usually very friendly and talkative once they know someone, this is not often the case with strangers. Unlike in the United States, where it is common to engage strangers in small talk, most Filipinos will not say a word to fill up the "quiet air" in an elevator, for example. If something strange or funny happens, though, there will always be a wisecracker or joker who will make a comment or two. Some will respond, but again, some will choose to simply keep quiet.

In contrast, Westerners who tend to value privacy express surprise at the questions Filipinos may ask them once they've been introduced. People may ask you where you are from or how many children you have. They might also ask about professional things, such as job titles and salaries. In some countries these questions would not be considered acceptable, but Filipinos in a social context may feel comfortable enough to ask them of visitors. If you are uncomfortable answering such personal questions, you may simply try to change the topic or perhaps direct the question to your new acquaintance.

It is also important to understand that what Filipinos say may not always convey what they really mean. Someone who replies *yes* to a request might simply mean that he or she will try to fulfill it, or may even be to shy to answer truthfully by saying *no*. Although *yes* often means *yes*, some Filipinos may say *yes* just to end a conversation or if they don't really understand what you are saying. If the answer to your question is critical, make sure the person you are talking to understands the importance of his or her answer, and that you want him or her to feel free to speak truthfully.

CHAPTER 11

Physical Etiquette

Although Western manners are generally acceptable in the Philippines it is important to understand a few key differences between the two cultures.

Filipinos communicate just as much in nonverbal ways as they do verbally. Together with words of respect, Filipinos also use gestures of respect. Especially in provincial areas, a child will greet his or her grandmother or another elderly person with a *mano*. This is simply a hand gesture in which a young person holds the hand of an older person and touches it to his or her forehead to receive the blessing of the older person.

It is not uncommon for Filipinos to greet each other with an embrace or a *beso*, a peck on the cheek. However, this is usually reserved for people they are very comfortable with, such as relatives and close friends. Good-byes may be treated similarly. A friendly hello or farewell with a wave of the hand is acceptable if you are uncomfortable with physical contact.

Facial expressions and body language sometimes indicate what people really feel, in spite of what they might be saying. Body language can be a helpful indication of the true feelings of Filipinos when they are not comfortable speaking their minds.

In instances when body language does not seem to agree with what an individual is saying, go ahead and ask nicely if he or she is sure about what is being said.

Filipinos may also answer questions in nonverbal ways. For example, if you ask them where the bathroom is, they will sometimes point toward it using their forefinger or their pouted lips rather than giving verbal directions. A nod of the head may also be used instead of the word *yes*, while a side-to-side movement of the head indicates a negative reply.

Foreigners should also be aware that the concept of "personal space" that is common in the West is not part of Filipino culture, at least outside of cosmopolitan cities like Manila or Cebu.

Since personal space is not an important part of Filipino etiquette, foreigners may be surprised by the way people squeeze together. This usually happens in high traffic areas and crowded churches, where during Sunday mass people will push into every inch of available pew space, potentially making the unsuspecting visitor uncomfortable. If you do not like too much physical contact it may be best to choose a less busy destination or attend mass early. When shopping in a mall, you may want to avoid the weekend crowd and go on a weekday instead. (There are a few upscale malls that do not get very full even on weekends.)

When using forms of mass transport in the Philippines, be prepared to be jammed together with strangers; drivers usually try to fill all the space in their vehicles. These drivers cannot raise fares without prior approval from the government, so this behavior is quite understandable given the low public transportation fares.

CHAPTER 12

The Use of Names

Filipinos are usually given a long formal first name and a shorter nickname. If born to a Catholic family, children are usually christened with names drawn from Christian tradition. The long history of Spanish influence in the Philippines can be seen in the many common names that have Spanish origins, such as *Maria* or *Juan*.

Formal first names are usually composed of two individual names. Instead of just *Juan*, a formal first name may be *Juan Antonio*. These two names can be helpful in telling apart people who have common names, such as *Maria* (which is later shortened to *Ma.*). You will be able to use second first names to distinguish between the women you meet named Maria—Ma. Lourdes, Ma. Cecilia, and Ma. Violeta. When she gets married, a woman will usually take the last name of her husband.

It is quite common for the first-born male to be named after his father. Some families even include Jose Sr. (senior), Jose Jr. (junior), and Jose III (the third). When the full name is written out this is indicated after an individual's last name, as with Jose Miguel Gatchalian, Sr.

Given the length of many Filipino names, it is also customary for parents to choose a shortened version of their child's name or a nickname that can be used in everyday conversation. This abbreviated name is given right after the baby is born, which may explain why some adults have cute or unusual nicknames, such as "Baby," or nicknames that are made up of a single syllable that is repeated, like Jun-Jun or Bing-Bing. Filipinos often continue to use these childlike nicknames even when they are adults in exalted or lofty positions.

Nicknames can be used for unofficial documents. When it comes to formal documentation, however, the formal name as registered on the birth certificate is usually used. When issuing a check or contract to someone you know as Toti, Jojo, or Leo, try to discover the individual's formal name. Sometimes the nickname will have no relation to the formal name, especially when the person goes by a moniker such as Bullet.

Another important thing to understand about names in the Philippines is that middle names are treated differently here. In the United States "middle name" usually refers to a second "first" name given to an individual at birth by his or her parents. But when asked for their middle names, Filipinos will usually provide their mother's maiden name. For example, if Maria Cristina's mom, Annie Reyes, is married to her dad, John Lastimosa, then Maria Cristina's full name will be Maria (first name) Cristina (second first name) Reyes (middle name) Lastimosa (last name).

While Filipinos tend to speak casually to their colleagues and friends, in business and formal situations people are usually addressed with their last names and a prefix of Mr, Ms, or Mrs.

Referring to someone using his or her surname only—"Come here, Santos!"—is considered rude in the Philippines. Unless you are a drill sergeant in the military trying to make your trainees quit, it is wise to avoid doing so.

If you forget someone's name, you can ask him or her in an apologetic manner to remind you what it is.

CHAPTER 13

The Use of Titles

In the Philippines, titles are often used in both professional and informal settings.

Filipinos even use a special title for each of their kin relations. As a foreigner, you are not expected to use these terms, but it helps to know what they mean. The eldest child in a family may be called *panganay*, *kuya*, or *ate*, while the youngest may be called *bunso*. Other commonly used titles for friends and family in the Philippines include *Ka*, *Tito*, *Tita*, *Lolo*, *Lola*, *Tatay*, *Nanay*, *Ninong*, *Ninang*, *Kumpare*, and *Kumare*. These words are most often used in an informal setting. *Ka*, which means "comrade" or "buddy," is used most often in the rural provinces. *Tito* and *Tita* mean "Uncle" and "Auntie" respectively, but they can also be also used for family friends who act like aunts or uncles. *Lolo* and *Lola* are "Grandpa" and "Grandma," while *Tatay* and *Nanay* are "Dad" and "Mom," respectively. *Ninong* and *Ninang* refer to a godfather or godmother in a wedding or baptism. *Kumpare* and *Kumare* is how godfathers and godmothers address one another. *Kuya* refers to an older brother; *Ate* refers to an older sister. *Pinsan* refers to a cousin.

Professional titles are also popular and may be used at even informal events such as parties. Lawyers like to be addressed as attorney, physicians as doctor, licensed engineers as engineer, military officers by their rank, and so on. These titles are often used without the addition of a surname in informal settings.

When a person retires from the judiciary, military, or diplomatic corps, they sometimes like to be addressed by their final (or retired) rank or position. Some former ambassadors still like to be called ambassador, or some former generals prefer to be addressed as such, even when they are actually civilians. For retirees, it is common to address them with the final title they attained in the workplace.

CHAPTER 14

Formal and Informal Introductions

Filipinos tend to be shy and may not feel comfortable making physical contact with people to whom they are being introduced. A nod of acknowledgement can usually be expected, although in business settings and in the cities the influence of American culture has led some locals to adopt the handshake as a method of introduction.

In a professional environment, the senior person will be introduced to the junior person and may offer him or her a handshake. If he is not her boss, a man waits for a woman to offer her hand. Business cards are also exchanged at initial meetings between colleagues.

In both personal and business life it is not uncommon to be introduced by someone rather than introducing yourself. Although it may sometimes be necessary to be more direct in your approach, many Filipinos are more comfortable with being introduced to new people by someone they know and trust.

In casual friendships, many foreigners will find that Filipinos are quite friendly and accommodating, though not necessarily outspoken. Filipinos adjust easily to other cultures and foreigners are likely to find that developing friendships with them happens quite naturally.

Most Filipinos value toughness and admire winners, but their hearts are most often with the underdog. That is why many *telenovelas* (long-running television series) feature heroes or heroines who start off oppressed but eventually win out. If you wish to happily meet and deal well with Filipinos, try to act confident, but not in an overt way. Filipinos do not like people who are "show-offs" or let their status in life go to their heads.

CHAPTER 15

Social Attire

Both Western and traditional Filipino clothing are regularly worn in the Philippines. Visitors will find that Western attire is appropriate in most situations, although on occasion Filipino dress will be welcomed, especially at formal events such as weddings. Torn jeans, tube tops, and other extremely casual or revealing clothing may be considered too scandalous for many places. Many restaurants follow a dress code.

For regular, day-to-day life, many Filipinos wear Western-style clothing. However, Filipinos are generally more conservative than their western counterparts and their clothes reflect this value accordingly. Their attire will depend on the weather, the activities they have planned for the day, and the level of formality associated with these activities. Unless you have been invited to attend a wedding or a similarly formal occasion most weekend events require smart casual clothing, which might include a dress or blouse and slacks for women and a button-down shirt, khakis, and leather shoes for men.

The traditional formal wear of the Philippines is the *barong tagalog* for men and the *terno* for women. The *barong tagalog* is the perfect formal wear for life in the Philippines, especially during the hot summers. It looks like a Western dress shirt, except that it is transparent and is not worn tucked in. Some historians have suggested that one reason for the *barong tagalog*'s translucency is that Filipinos were forbidden to carry weapons during the Spanish era, and these nearly see-through shirts made it difficult to hide them.

Today the *barong tagalog* is often worn over a *camison,* or cotton shirt, with slacks and leather shoes. *Barong tagalog* are usually made from processed *jusi* (pronounced *husi*) or banana fibers. For more expensive versions, *piña* (pronounced *pinya*) cloth made of pineapple fibers is used.

Women may wear the *terno to* formal events. This national costume was popularized in the international scene by former First Lady Imelda Marcos. One would often see her wearing a *terno* with the signature butterfly sleeves and long gown designed by different couturiers.

Filipino women may instead opt to wear an elaborate traditional costume known as *Maria Clara* to formal events. This dress is named after a female character in the novels of the Philippine national hero Dr. Jose Rizal. Maria Clara was believed to be the epitome of the Filipino woman: conservative, dainty, and well-mannered. The Maria Clara is an adaptation of women's clothing common during the Spanish era, which included the *panuelo* (a shawl or wrap) and *saya* (long skirt). Vintage necklaces and Spanish fans are also part of the outfit. Some Filipino brides choose wedding dresses based on this design.

Most wedding invitations will specify the type of attire to be worn. This is usually formal or semi-formal wear, or sometimes native garb. Out of respect for the couple, you should arrive properly dressed. Unless specifically mentioned or implied, most invitations that request formal attire do not necessarily mean that women must wear traditional Filipino dress or long gowns, or that men should appear in tuxedos. Cocktail or evening dresses are generally appropriate formal attire for women, while men might wear business suits or *barong tagalog*. Semi-formal attire is a bit more relaxed than formal wear, though not as relaxed as smart casual wear.

Baptisms are usually held during the day and the required attire may be anything from semi-formal to smart casual. Sunday mass is also considered an important event and wearing your Sunday best is something that is admired and respected. (Not everyone manages to do so every week, though.)

Due to the hot weather and sometimes economic constraints, many Filipinos settle for comfortable though not necessarily fancy or trendy clothes. It is uncommon to see high fashion in the streets. However, the country is also known for its talented fashion designers and the Filipino love of fashion is evident during private events hosted by affluent groups or during business affairs. Among the members of the upper class, you are bound to find many expensively and well-dressed men and women.

In work settings, clothing is similar to what one might wear in the West. The country's hot climate, however, sometimes makes it impractical to wear complete suits unless one is attending a formal business meeting, which would generally be held in an air-conditioned venue. Otherwise, male professionals settle for either long-sleeved dress shirts and ties or long- or short-sleeved *barong tagalog*. In informal settings, short-sleeved polo shirts will do. Women may choose from business suits, dresses, or smart casual wear depending on the type of industry they work in.

CHAPTER 16

Dining Etiquette

Unless you are attending a formal function in a hotel or a reception hall, most meals in the Philippines are informal or casual and don't require any special etiquette. There are really no rituals involved, except that most Filipinos prefer to eat with someone rather than sit alone at a table. When in a group, a prayer is sometimes said before meals. Typical Western customs—such as not taking too much food or burping at the table—are also observed here.

Western-style table settings are common at formal and business meals in the Philippines, with a fork, spoon, and knife provided for each diner. In less formal situations Filipinos are quite accustomed to eating with only a spoon and fork, using the fork to push food onto the spoon. And because Japanese and Chinese restaurants abound, the use of chopsticks is quite widespread.

In rural areas, however, eating with the hands is common. It is quite possible that your host will invite you to sample some of the Philippines' traditional dishes. He or she may bring you to a restaurant where customers eat with their hands. If you are uncomfortable using your hands, you can request a spoon and fork.

Before eating with your hands you may be given a clean, hot towel or, more likely, be asked to wash your hands in a sink near the table.

There is a basic strategy for eating with your hands: Take food from the plate using the tips of your fingers and use your thumb to push the food into your mouth. Never let the food touch the palm of your hand, which can be messy. You can also get tips from your Filipino dining partners or watch how they handle the situation

Logically, foods such as pasta, soup, and salad are not suitable for eating with the hands. Your host should be able to anticipate this and provide plates, bowls, and utensils for food that cannot be eaten this way. Traditionally, food eaten with the hands is served on a clean banana leaf. Many native restaurants present food in this manner, or use a banana leaf as a plate liner. Consider this leaf a disposable plate.

Food may be served buffet or family style, or delivered to each diner by a waiter. During a buffet meal, do not be surprised if some Filipinos go to the buffet table and get their appetizer, main course, and dessert at the same time and bring them all to their table at once. This saves them trips to the buffet. It is also acceptable to get your appetizer first, return for your main course, and then go back for dessert.

The country's delicacies include *lechon*, or roasted pig. The skin is usually crunchy and is a favorite of many Filipinos. Day-old leftover *lechon* is transformed into *paksiw na lechon* (*lechon* cooked with liver sauce) or *pritchon* (fried *lechon*). In the more modern areas of the country *pritchon* has become a gourmet dish created by wrapping the *pritchon* and a green vegetable like celery in pita bread, which is then served with different dipping sauces such as honey mustard or garlic mayonnaise. It is a party favorite and a must-try for the visiting foreigner.

Other local delicacies include *balut* (boiled duck egg with a partially developed fetus inside) or *penoy* (boiled fertilized duck egg). Not everyone will take to the idea of eating a duck fetus; feel free to decline if the dish is too exotic for your taste. You can also decline the frog legs that are served in some restaurants if that dish does not sit well with your stomach.

Staple dishes served in most homes include *tinola* (chicken with ginger and fish-sauce broth) and *sinigang* (soup with sour tamarind flavor). You may wish to try these dishes if you have a preference for soup-based meals. As with most Asian countries, rice is a staple and is served with almost all meals.

For dessert, a popular treat is the *halo-halo*: a mixture of ice, milk, sugar, and about seven different sweet items including *leche flan* (custard), *ube* (yam), *nata de coco* (coconut gelatin), chick peas, brown beans, and so on. All these ingredients are quite popular with kids and very easy for adults to appreciate, too. The ingredients may also be eaten separately.

Other dessert options include the many mouth-watering, native-grown fruits that you may wish to sample. Popular choices among foreigners include the green and yellow mango, banana, melon, watermelon, strawberry, tangerine (known locally as *ponkan*), and pineapple. More exotic but likewise delicious choices include lanzones, rambutan, mangosteen, jackfruit (known as *langka* in the Philippines), durian, and others. Keep in mind that the durian has a strong (some say obnoxious) odor and may not be appealing to people who aren't used to it. Loyal fans swear to its great taste, though.

If you have specific dietary concerns (such as following halal or kosher practices, needing diabetic-friendly meals, and so on), don't hesitate to inform your host or hotel or restaurant managers. Be prepared to bring any specific food items you may need, such as kosher salt, because they may not be available in stores.

For example, most Filipinos simply use rock or table salt and will have no clue what kosher salt is.

Diabetics and heart patients may have to watch what they eat because certain Filipino dishes are high in cholesterol. However, Filipinos are usually more than willing to accommodate their guests' health and food restrictions by suggesting or providing healthier dishes. There are many different cuisines served in restaurants and hotels throughout the Philippines; making a healthy choice should not prove to be too difficult.

Chapter 17

Paying the Bill

Filipinos usually go to great lengths to entertain their guests. Even if doing so will cause financial hardship, they may still insist on paying the bill when you visit restaurants or bars together. A meal that might not seem particularly special or extravagant to most foreigners may be the equivalent of a Filipino host's daily wage. Sensitivity to the host's financial situation would be appropriate. Depending on the verbal and body language cues your host is giving, you might insist on paying or going Dutch. When dining with friends, it is usually expected that you will split the bill unless the invitation was for a special occasion such as a birthday party. When socializing with affluent hosts or at business events it is usually the one who issued the invitation who foots the bill. Relax and just enjoy the meal.

The tip or service charge in most restaurants is 10 percent, which will be added to your bill along with the 12 percent value-added tax levied by the government. Mindful of the low salaries of most waiters, some diners choose to leave an additional tip, especially when the service rendered was very good. Most waiters are kind and will appreciate this tip, but try to leave paper money rather than small coins.

Not all restaurants include the service charge in the bill so it is a good idea to check the details. If the service charge is not included, a minimum tip of 10 percent would be appreciated.

Filipinos use a special hand gesture to request their bill at restaurants: after they have caught the eye of their waiter, they extend a hand and move their thumb and index finger in the shape of a rectangle. This maneuver can also be done using both hands. Instead of saying "waiter," Filipinos will sometimes say "boss!" to get their waiter's attention. This is somewhat acceptable in casual encounters, but you should never resort to "psst" or "hoy," which are considered impolite. And as Americans love to say, "Hay is for horses," so avoid using the word *hey*, especially in phrases such as "Hey you."

Shopping is a popular activity for tourists in the Philippines because many goods can actually be purchased at a low price. A lot of malls carry popular international brands and cheaper local brands. Stores may charge the standard international price for imported items, but it is more likely that you will pay two to three times more than this standard price unless there is a big sale. Cheaper alternatives are also available: many local and foreign-brand clothes, for example, may be sold at very low prices. Just be aware that cheap foreign-brand items might be export overruns or imitations, thus accounting for the rock bottom prices. These items may not be the best buy, so you should check both quality and price.

When purchasing major appliances, remember to ask about a warranty or after-sale service. Often, stores will ask you to keep your receipt together with the warranty card. It would also be a good idea to ask where the service centers are located in case the appliance breaks down. Some service centers are in hard-to-find areas, so it would be best to be informed ahead of time where they are.

In addition to shopping malls, there is also the option of visiting a *tiangge* (flea market), where various goods can be purchased at a bargain. Some haggling is often expected. Sellers usually expect the buyer to ask for what is known as *tawad na presyo*, or "bargain price." A successful bargaining strategy is to ask for the seller's best price. You can reply with a lower offer, although the seller will usually then give reasons why that price is unacceptable. After haggling for a while, you will eventually agree on a price that is somewhere between the seller's best price and your *tawad* price.

Always watch your belongings when visiting crowded flea markets and even malls. Snatchers and pickpockets are always on the lookout for people they can victimize. You may also wish to ask your host which areas are safer and less hazardous for tourists.

Credit cards are usually accepted in urban areas in the Philippines, although you may wish to limit the use of your card to reputable establishments such as nationwide chains or well-known stores. (Note that charges in a foreign currency may incur extra fees from your credit card company.) Cash is also used often and it may be good to carry enough for your needs. You can exchange your money at the bank, money changer (usually found in malls or business districts), or at any SM department store nationwide.

CHAPTER 18

Home-Visiting Etiquette

Filipinos are less hesitant than Americans to invite people into their homes and are usually willing to entertain visitors even on short notice. However, it is always best to give advance notice when you are visiting.

Filipino homes are like American homes in that they usually have a living room to entertain visitors, a dining room, bedrooms, bathrooms, kitchen and probably a laundry area. Condominiums compress some of these areas and the living room will sometimes also act as the dining area. You may be asked to remove your shoes at the main door of any homes you visit, but this is not common. Meals are typically eaten at Western-style tables.

Most Filipinos have a knack for making people feel welcome in their homes. They do not expect you to bring anything along when you visit, but food or beverages are welcome additions at any gathering. Food that goes well with the meal is especially appreciated, so feel free to check in with your host about what might be best to bring. Many people choose to bring a dessert. You may also bring a bottle of wine, but only if you think that your hosts actually drink the beverage. For potluck parties, of course, the host may assign you a dish to bring.

When visiting secluded or out-of-the-way areas, it may be wise to arrange in advance for the return trip to your hotel to avoid imposing on your host for transportation. Hosts may volunteer to bring you back to wherever you are staying, especially if they have their own car, but don't count on it. Feel free to accept a ride home with other guests if you are comfortable with the idea. Otherwise, you may want to hire a car service for the day so you can leave at the appropriate moment.

There are some areas in the Philippines that do not have good roads. Check a map when planning a home visit and ask around for suggestions or ideas about the location.

Facilities in the provinces are not always as modern as they are in the cities and being prepared for any eventuality is smart. If you are not sure about your accommodations, you may wish to bring your own towel, slippers, soap, shampoo, toothbrush, toothpaste, and bottled water for drinking and brushing your teeth. Sometimes, especially if visiting far-flung or remote provinces, you may also need to bring your own bed sheets, pillowcases, and even pillows, as well as snacks that can get you by in case the food served is too exotic for your taste. Also have a first-aid kit ready for any emergency.

If possible, borrow or buy a cell phone to facilitate communication. In some provinces things such as phones, electricity, and water are not widely available. Keep important phone numbers listed. Inform your primary host of your whereabouts or cell phone number so you may be easily reached in case of an emergency.

CHAPTER 19

Public Etiquette

M odesty is an important aspect of public etiquette in the Philippines. Filipinos usually behave in a subdued way, and expect that foreigners do the same. Wild activities such as flashing and streaking are not popular in the country. Public displays of emotion are not encouraged. This includes both love and anger. However, particularly in the cities, the influence of Western movies, songs, and television shows has somewhat compromised the tradition of modesty.

Behavior that might be considered acceptable in the West is sometimes inappropriate in the Philippines, such as public displays of affection. Most Filipinos are uncomfortable with public displays of affection. A woman who has too much physical contact with a man she has just met may be perceived as a loose woman. *Delicadeza* or "propriety" is a virtue attributed to people who conduct themselves well and show good manners. It is also used to refer to those who are sensitive to the moral principles or human values of the people around them. A person with *delicadeza* is considered to have integrity.

As in many parts of the world, visitors to economically depressed areas will sometimes hear heated arguments that the whole neighborhood may be aware of in spite of the Filipino appreciation for quiet modesty. Some people can also be melodramatic and may publicly display anger or rage when they lose control. These sudden outbursts happen precisely because many Filipinos tend to suppress their emotions, so when they do lose control the results can be scandalous or destructive.

During public events, Filipinos are more likely to blend in with the crowd than call attention to themselves. This tendency can be seen at conferences and seminars, where it may take a while for the speaker to get the audience to ask questions. This is due to shyness as well as the desire to fit in and not be at odds with other people. It is this sense of belonging that keeps Filipinos from doing anything completely against the group consensus.

The Filipino word *pakikisama* indicates that conforming to a group is more important than the desires of an individual. While there will always be mavericks who don't seem to care about what other people say, most Filipinos value the opinions of others. Because Filipinos are group-oriented rather than individualistic, they are mindful of how their actions will affect their kin, their close friends, their employer, and any organizations they belong to.

Prudence and common sense should also be exercised in public areas. Due to reported cases of kidnapping in the news, some parents may be wary of strangers. If you are in a public place and see a young child playing, do not immediately approach the child and strike up a conversation, no matter how innocent your intentions may be. You can get into trouble with authorities and bystanders—not to mention the child's parents. However, there may be times when spontaneous conversation would be perfectly acceptable, such as when the child is in the presence of his or her parents or guardians, and their behavior toward you is friendly.

Visitors who smoke should also be aware that in certain areas in Manila, particularly in the business district, there is a law that prohibits smoking in enclosed public establishments such as air-conditioned malls. When in a public place, it is best to find an area designated for smoking. Some establishments, such as coffee shops, actually provide separate smoking areas. If you are unsure where that place may be, you can simply ask the locals.

CHAPTER 20

Filipino Fiestas

Fiestas in the Philippines originated with the celebration of Catholic feast days. Fiestas might also mark the end of the harvest season or other special events. Fiestas are usually festive occasions with lots of food and drink. This is a time when the whole community throws its doors open to visitors.

Whether they are locals or foreigners, everyone is invited to join in the celebration. There is no real ceremony; you simply go from house to house and partake of the feasts that willing residents have prepared.

The best way for visiting foreigners to enjoy a fiesta is to go with a trusted local who can bring them around. If you really must go by yourself, always be cautious and don't be too trusting of strangers. Make sure that you arrange your transportation to and from the town that you will visit prior to reaching your destination. You may also wish to stay at a local hotel or inn, or perhaps at the home of a good friend who lives nearby. Always have a contingency plan in case things don't go as you hoped. In the Philippines, bringing a cell phone is a natural thing to do, because changes in plans caused by traffic or car trouble are common occurrences.

During fiestas, you might enter several private homes of locals who have prepared feasts for their visitors. When you plan to attend a fiesta, it is wise to avoid eating and drinking before going. Some hosts will feel offended if you do not eat or drink with them when you enter their homes. Eat and drink sparingly in each house—unless you want to end up stuffed like a turkey.

If you see a group of people drinking, you may be offered a *tagay* ("shot") of either beer or hard liquor. Unless you are a teetotaler, go ahead and take the shot but then excuse yourself immediately if you don't want to end up in a lengthy drinking session that you might regret later. Another option is to politely decline the drink, citing health or other reasons.

It is also worthy of note that in certain unsafe neighborhoods foreigners have been scammed into gulping a drink laced with a drug or other controlled substance. The drugged foreigner is then robbed of his or her credit card and belongings. These incidents can happen at any time of the year, not just during fiestas, so it is always best to be cautious when accepting food and drink. Traveling with a reliable companion and guide is highly recommended.

For many people—particularly those who come from the provinces—the celebration of a fiesta in their hometown is a very big event. Vacation leave is often planned around fiestas to allow people who have moved away from their hometowns to return. Do not be surprised if Filipino employees request time off to go home to the provinces during fiesta season.

CHAPTER 21

Other Celebrations

Filipinos love to celebrate life, and annual religious events and special lifecycle events provide ample opportunity for them to do so.

In the Philippines, Christmas is the most celebrated holiday of the year, and Filipinos are known for the importance that they give to the Christmas season. As early as September, you may be surprised to find that some radio stations are already playing Christmas songs.

There are many traditions surrounding the season, including *Simbang Gabi*. This is the custom of Filipino Catholics to attend dawn masses daily starting on 16 December. It is considered a major achievement to attend all of the masses, which culminate with the *Misa de Gallo* (midnight mass) that marks Christmas Day. Attending these masses—which in some parishes begin as early as 4 AM each day—is seen as sacrifice done for a spiritual good. *Noche Buena,* another important Christmas tradition in the Philippines, is the feast or midnight celebration that follows the *Misa de Gallo*.

Another important celebration in the lives of many Filipino girls and their families is a debutante party. When a young woman reaches eighteen years of age, her family sponsors a celebration during which she is introduced to society. Prior to the event, the debutante usually takes great pains to have a formal gown prepared and spends time practicing the first dance with her court, which is composed of both male and female friends. The event is usually held in a big hotel or restaurant, and guests are expected to come in formal attire. The debutante's father usually has the first dance with her and her brother has the second, after which she dances with the other young men who were invited. This is called the dance of the eighteen roses, during which the debutante will dance with eighteen men (including her father and brothers) who will each give her a red rose.

If the family cannot afford such a grand introduction, this traditional party may be omitted in favor of a simpler celebration. In wealthy families the celebrant will sometimes opt for a car or other expensive item in lieu of the debutante party.

Other events that Filipino families normally celebrate include graduations from elementary school, high school, and college; the passing of professional licensure or bar examinations; and other personal and professional milestones. Celebrations can range from simple family dinners to expensive parties at well-known establishments.

In addition to Christmas, Christians celebrate baptisms and marriages in a grand manner. The season leading up to Easter is also observed. On Ash Wednesday, the first day of Lent, you will see many people with ashes on their foreheads. For serious Catholics, Ash Wednesday and Good Friday are days of fasting and abstinence from meat, so don't be surprised if you are served seafood or vegetable dishes on these days. Holy Week is usually a break from work when time is spent with family. People in the provinces still practice what is known as *Pabasa* ("reading"), during which all the verses of the Bible relating to the passion, death, and resurrection of Christ are sung. Other common

Lenten practices include *Visita Iglesia* ("church visit") on Holy Thursday, when Filipino families go to at least seven churches to give homage to the Eucharist, or the body of Christ, which is exposed on that day. During Good Friday, there is a "washing of the feet" that is usually dramatized in the church along with a ritual that includes kissing the crucifix. Black Saturday (also known as Holy Saturday) is usually a quiet day intended to be spent in anticipation of Easter Sunday, which is the following day. For serious Catholics, Easter Sunday is the most important day of the year. However, commercialization of this holiday has brought with it many distractions from what was meant to be a solemn time. For example, some people decide to go out of town and stay in beach resorts, while those who remain in the city end up going to the malls, which usually open at noon on holidays.

CHAPTER 22

Dating, Courtship, and Engagement

Although romantic relationships in the Philippines are conducted in ways similar to romantic relationships in the West, this conservative nation also has its own unique traditions when it comes to love. Unmarried Filipino couples sometimes decide to live together, but this arrangement is frowned upon. Most people still see marriage as the ultimate goal of any romantic relationship. While arranged marriages may still occur, most Filipinos want to personally choose their lifetime companions.

In the Philippines, the dating scene differs from the courtship stage in terms of the formality of the relationship and the intention of the couple. The dating stage is considered a time for getting to know someone and the couple is not bound by any commitment. It is also possible that a young woman will only be allowed to go out on dates if accompanied by a chaperone.

People who are dating aren't usually considered boyfriend and girlfriend. Instead, it is seen as a most opportune time for both parties to discover whether they are interested in moving beyond the friendship level. At this point, a woman may be open to meeting as many men as possible in order to help discern who would be best for her.

It is more often the man who makes the first move in setting dates. He will often plan and arrange the whole event and foot the bill. He may even be offended if the woman insists on splitting the bill. Filipino men are generally known for their gallantry toward women, most especially when they are in the courtship phase of a relationship. It is quite common to see a man opening doors for a woman, paying for their meal while out on the town, or offering to bring his date home, especially if it is late at night or she must travel through an unsafe neighborhood. During the courtship stage a Filipino man often states or manifests his intention to win the heart of a woman he is attracted to or has feelings for.

In the provinces and more conservative areas in the country, dating is not common. In these rural areas, a Filipino man usually decides to pursue and woo a woman through *harana,* or singing a love song to his beloved. The man's close friends may accompany him to the woman's house, where they will sing a few songs, usually while standing beneath a window. Normally, the woman and her family look on, amused, before inviting the man into the house. But if the woman is not interested in the man's advances, she may not listen at all or keep her windows and doors closed.

Another traditional practice in the provinces and rural areas is *paninilbihan,* or "service." This is when a prospective groom is required by the woman's family to do some chores around their house to prove his sincerity and worth. Tasks may include chopping wood, fetching water, or other household chores. However, this practice is fast disappearing and is virtually nonexistent in the big cities.

A suitor may ask a Filipino woman, or a Filipina, if she is interested in going steady. While a traditional Filipina may be interested in a suitor, she may hesitate to give a direct and immediate response. If she says "maybe," it means that the man may continue courting her to show that he is really serious about pursuing her. But if she keeps adamantly saying "no", she is probably not interested in him. A suitor should be well aware that a Filipina usually needs to have trust in the man courting her and needs to see that he has serious intentions for her. Traditional Filipinas do not take love, courtship, and marriage lightly.

The relationship is usually formalized after the woman accepts the man's proposal to develop an exclusive relationship with him by saying *oo*, or "yes." At this point the couple is considered boyfriend and girlfriend, or simply steadies. During this stage the couple gets the opportunity to get to know each other better in order to discern whether they are right for marriage.

A Filipino man will likely propose marriage during a fancy dinner or some other formal date, and he may present an engagement ring. If the woman accepts, the man is eventually expected to bring his family to meet her family in a ceremony called the *pamanhikan*. This can be very important, because both immediate and extended families (and even quasi-relatives) are fundamental to the lives of Filipinos. A Filipino marriage is just as much a marriage of two families as of two individuals. When you marry a Filipino, you also marry into his or her family.

Brides from middle-class and affluent families are given a lavish party known as a *despedida de soltera,* or bridal shower, a few days before the wedding. It is an occasion for the bride to invite her friends and family to a gathering that commemorates her last few days as a single woman.

In the past, the families of both bride and groom would have had a big say in how the wedding looked. Nowadays, though, input from the bride's and groom's families is considered, but it is usually the couple that takes the lead in planning the wedding. They may even hire a professional wedding coordinator if they can afford one.

Traditionally, the groom's family took care of wedding expenses, but today more modern couples save up from their own incomes in order to manage their wedding budget. Given the economic situation, however, their families usually chip in for whatever is lacking.

Big weddings are common in the Philippines because marriage is essentially viewed as a social event and an opportunity for the community to witness the union. The whole event is planned to perfection. Depending on the budget, this planning might include having formal invitations printed; hiring a hotel, restaurant, or caterer to serve food; getting a dressmaker or designer to create clothes for the whole wedding party; planning floral arrangements; hiring musicians for the event; and so on. Many hotels and other establishments offer package deals that may even include special arrangements for the bridal car (usually a luxury sedan or limousine) or include the wedding cake.

The wedding party is usually made up of a maid of honor and a best man, as well as several bridesmaids, groomsmen, flower girls, and ring bearers. Men who are invited to be part of the wedding entourage usually wear a coat and tie or a *barong tagalog* paired with black or dark slacks. Women in the entourage normally agree to have their dresses coordinated and sewn by one designer so they will all be wearing the same color and style of dress.

Weddings are typically formal and invitations require an RSVP. Some Filipinos are not adept at confirming their attendance for such events, so someone needs to follow up to ask for confirmation from the people who have been invited.

For Catholics, the wedding ceremony is usually celebrated with a mass. Along with the usual mass rites, a typical Filipino wedding includes the placing of a veil over the bride's head to signify her submission to her husband; the placing of a white cloth cord around the necks of the groom and bride (as if they were wearing a connected necklace) to signify their union; and the lighting of two candles. At the reception, the couple sets free two white doves, shares a piece of the wedding cake, and drinks wine together. At the end of the reception, the bride throws her wedding bouquet and it is said the woman who catches it will walk down the aisle soon.

CHAPTER 23

Gift Giving

In the Philippines, gift giving is an important part of social relationships. For many Filipinos, though, it is the thought that counts and not the amount spent to purchase the gift. Appreciation or love is shown with the thoughtfulness with which the gift was made or chosen, and not its cost.

Christmas is the country's most celebrated season and gift giving is expected. Traditionally, families attend the *Misa de Gallo* (Christmas Eve mass starting at around 8 or 10 PM) and then have their *Noche Buena,* or Christmas Eve dinner, before midnight. The exchange and opening of gifts happens at the stroke of midnight. Filipino families may celebrate Christmas Eve differently, but a special dinner and the giving of gifts are usually included.

Aguinaldo is a local term for monetary Christmas gifts given to children by godparents or older people. The *aguinaldo* often takes the form of new paper bills. On Christmas day, especially in rural areas, parents with their children in tow visit relatives, close friends, and their children's godparents and expect some kind of *aguinaldo* for the small ones. The amount may range from P20 to P500 (fifty cents US to ten US dollars), depending on the resources and generosity of the giver. Sometimes, the money is placed inside a small envelope for discretion.

In certain business settings gifts may be inappropriate, particularly expensive ones. Extravagant gifts may be construed as bribes, as in the case of suppliers giving expensive gifts to corporate purchasing officers. In addition, the giving of expensive gifts by bosses to their subordinates may imply favoritism.

Because expensive gifts may be seen as bribes in business settings, token gifts are the rule rather than the exception. Companies may give calendars or baskets of fruit to their customers and suppliers during the Christmas holidays. The type of gift will depend on the size and industry of the company. Corporate gifts are also given to speakers at events and to participants in special events and sponsored occasions.

During Christmas, many companies allow their employees to hold Kris Kringle or Secret Santa events. Each employee draws the name of another employee to whom they will anonymously give one token gift each day, without revealing their identity until the official revelation, which generally happens during the company's Christmas party. Some companies limit this celebration to an exchange of gifts during the Christmas party.

If you are staying long in the Philippines and have a driver, maid, nanny, or other domestic employee, giving them each a gift during the Christmas season would be well appreciated.

Employers are also mandated by law to give their workers a thirteenth-month bonus equaling to one month's salary. Employers are usually thoughtful enough to give the thirteenth-month payment by mid-December to allow employees time to shop for the holidays. In addition to bonus pay, a variety of goods such as canned goods, hams, or baskets of fruit are distributed to many Filipino employees during this season.

Aside from the Christmas season, regular occasions such as birthdays, baptisms, and weddings are also opportunities to give gifts. Many couples, particularly in the cities, take advantage of bridal gift registries to indicate the types of gifts that they would like to receive. Gift registries can be created for baptisms as well, although these are not yet common. Gifts for birthdays are usually tailored to the personality of the receiver. At parties, people sometimes throw coins into the air for the kids (and adults) to grab. This kind of activity lends a festive mood to the occasion but may also hurt the little ones in the process.

Although it is the thought that counts when giving a gift, try not to give a recycled gift back to the same person who gave it to you. This is needless to say, but it does happen. You should also avoid giving food that spoils easily.

Gift-wrapping need not be fancy or expensive. There are no strict rules in gift giving except that the gift should match the character or need of the receiver.

CHAPTER 24

Visiting Places of Worship

There are many historic churches and mosques in the Philippines that are worth visiting, some of which date back to the Spanish era. When visiting a church or other place of worship, remember that it is primarily a place of worship and only secondarily an architectural masterpiece and tourist attraction. Proper decorum should be practiced when visiting and taking pictures.

When you enter a Catholic church, keep in mind that the most sacred place is the tabernacle where the Eucharist is kept. You can easily spot the tabernacle because it usually stands behind or near the altar and is always lit with a candle or lamp. This light signifies that there is Eucharist inside the tabernacle. The custom on entering a church is to face the tabernacle while genuflecting, or deeply bending one knee and bowing your head. As a sign of respect, Catholics are supposed to genuflect every time they pass in front of the tabernacle, which is the reason why some care must be taken when trying to take pictures by the altar. Non-Catholics may also genuflect out of respect, but they may not participate in Communion as that is reserved for practicing Catholics.

You should be discreet in your movements within the church to avoid distracting those who are there to worship. Avoid taking pictures if there is a mass going on. Even if there is no mass, Catholics may still be praying inside the church. If you wish to take pictures, you should do so discreetly. Many Filipinos take their faith seriously and are upset if tourists do not respect the sanctity of their place of worship. You might want to ask for permission before you take photos, preferably from a member of the clergy or a caretaker. You might also consider taking pictures when no churchgoer is around.

The highest point of the celebration of mass is the Consecration. This is when the priest raises the bread and wine to be transformed into the body and blood of Jesus Christ. A bell accompanies the lifting of the bread and wine, and you will find most of those attending mass in a kneeling position. If you are not Catholic, you may just sit or stand and watch quietly. At this point, everyone in the church is expected to stop any kind of activity as a sign of respect. Even those collecting offertory money will remain still until the Consecration is over. You may resume movement when you see people stand up from their kneeling position. However, since the mass is still ongoing, you should try not to make noise or distract churchgoers.

CHAPTER 25

Attending a Wake

Wakes in the Philippines normally last for a few days, during which families, friends, and acquaintances keep each other company while mourning the loss of a loved one. Depending on the social status of the deceased, the wake or *lamay* may take place in a home, funeral parlor, church, basketball court, or even in a tent erected in the middle of the street in front of the home of the deceased.

Paying your respects is very much appreciated here, and your grieving Filipino friend will remember you for the gesture of attending their loved one's wake. Normally, you do not need a formal invitation to attend a wake. Once you hear of the sad news and when and where the wake will be held, you should feel free to attend. Visiting hours may be from as early as 9 AM to as late as 11 PM or even later. Many people go to a wake straight from their respective places of work. Remember that the immediate family will probably accompany the dead unceasingly, which means that a member of the family has to remain at the wake twenty-four hours a day. A shifting schedule for this is usually agreed on among family members.

When attending the first few days of the wake, go in casual attire; there is no need to dress up, but you should not wear slippers, shorts, or anything revealing. On the day of the burial itself, however, wear smart casual clothes, such as a polo shirt, slacks, and leather shoes. If you are quite close to the deceased or part of the immediate family, more formal attire would be appropriate, such as a *barong tagalog* and dark slacks for a man or a dress for a woman. Black is the most acceptable color to wear, although white is also growing in popularity. Bright colors such as red, yellow, or orange are usually avoided because they do not fit in with the mood of mourning. Subdued colors are more appropriate.

Snack food is normally served during the wake. If the death has come as an unexpected shock (such as in a car accident or as the result of a crime), expect the wake to be a solemn event. However, if the death was expected because the deceased was very old or had suffered from a long illness, the atmosphere will probably be less solemn.

Because many Filipino families include one or more individuals who work or live abroad, it is customary for the grieving family to wait for the distant family members to come home to pay their respects before the body is buried. Some might choose to end the wake after as few as two or three days to bury the dead or cremate them if there are reasons for doing so, such as communicable diseases.

If you cannot attend a wake, you may send flowers (unless the bereaved request otherwise through newspaper obituaries) or send a mass card (for Catholics).

After the burial the bereaved family holds a nine-day prayer vigil in their home, but mourning in the Philippines generally lasts for up to forty days. People in mourning avoid attending festive celebrations or observe these occasions with a little more solemnity than usual. Some widows, widowers, or immediate family members may continue to wear a small, rectangular, black pin on their chests to signify that they are still in mourning, sometimes even beyond the forty days. On the fortieth day after the burial, some families choose to get together to essentially mark the end of mourning.

November 1 (All Saints' Day) and November 2 (All Souls' Day) are days that families remember all of their relatives who have passed away. During these November holidays, whole families troop to cemeteries not only to place candles or flowers on the graves or mausoleums of deceased family members, but also to spend some time at the cemetery with their living relatives and have a picnic inside cemetery grounds. Some people take this occasion less seriously than others, and the atmosphere may take on a festive mood with loud music playing in the background and gambling going on. Some people avoid visiting the cemetery on the aforementioned dates precisely because of the expected crowd, which could swell to thousands. They might instead choose to visit cemeteries before or after November 1.

CHAPTER 26

Exploring the Countryside

The Philippines has 7,107 islands for visitors to explore, offering every imaginable entertainment: shopping, golfing or playing tennis, lounging on the beach, and scuba or skin diving. Each province has its own special attractions.

For those who want to experience the nightlife in the Philippines, the expatriate community generally hangs out in expensive bars and restaurants in urban areas and resorts in Manila and Cebu. These places can be just as hip as those in international cities such as New York or London. If you want to try some of the local hangouts that are not frequented by foreigners, it would probably be best to go with a trusted local friend who knows the area and can help translate for you.

The people you meet in the cities and semi-urban areas are likely to be very accustomed to dealing with foreigners and quite familiar with Western ways, but the rural population tends to be more traditional and conservative than their urban counterparts. If you travel off the beaten path, however, the hospitable Filipino nature might just reward you with an unparalleled experience of a unique rural culture that revolves around friendliness and generosity.

A trip to the provinces means some quiet time away from hectic city life and an opportunity to think of anything other than work. A world apart, you can discover seaside retreats prefect for relaxation, where you can select your own freshly caught fish or seafood and watch it be prepared right in front of you—all for a very low price.

However, there are things to consider when traveling in rural areas. If you are going on a road trip and wish to use a bathroom, your best bet is to go to an establishment with a clearly displayed Department of Tourism seal of approval, or any well-known fast-food chain or restaurant that has found its way into the rural areas. You may also find clean bathrooms in gas stations. Should you find yourself in a place with a clean bathroom, you might as well use it because the next one you encounter may not be as clean. It is also advisable to bring your own soap and tissue; not all bathrooms provide these amenities.

Depending on the price you are prepared to pay, lodging may be at a five-star hotel or a bed-and-breakfast. Check out the facilities and the room before deciding. When pricing comes up at bed-and-breakfasts, you can sometimes haggle.

It may be wise to hire a tour guide if you are exploring the Philippines for the first time or are by yourself. This service might be provided by your hotel or listed in the yellow pages. Some rental car drivers may also double as tour guides. Just be sure to check the background of the individual or company that you hire to guide or help you. Some unsuspecting tourists have been swindled because they were too trusting.

In general, Filipinos are very friendly and will go out of their way to please you and ensure your enjoyment and safety. However, this is not the case in all areas, so talk to your host if you have one and—most importantly—be cautious.

CHAPTER 27

Public Transportation

The best option for getting around in the Philippines is often to have a local friend drive you. You might offer to pay for gas, particularly for long trips. If you are not traveling on a budget another option is to rent a car with a driver, so that in effect your driver becomes your tour guide. You could also invite your local friends to go along with you on such a trip.

You may not want to rent a car and drive it yourself unless you have been in the Philippines for some time. For many visitors, the experience of driving around Philippine cities is almost like a roller-coaster ride (unless you get stuck in heavy traffic and are forced to move at an excruciatingly slow pace). Ill-mannered drivers who make right turns from the left lane, drive through red lights, or swerve from lane to lane may catch you off guard. Also, the Philippines has a lot of traffic rules that may not seem to make sense.

In many situations, it may be wise to consider taking public transportation. Public mass transport may be run by the government or private companies. Before you attempt to go anywhere, try to get clear instructions from a local on what mode of transportation to take, where to take it from, and when is the best time to take it.

However you plan to travel, dress for comfort and never openly display valuables or expensive items. If you must carry an expensive item such as a laptop it is recommended that you rent a car with a driver or take a taxi. When riding in public vehicles, try to have bills in smaller denominations or coins for paying your fare to avoid the potential hassle of needing change. If people seem friendly you can certainly try to make small talk, but don't push your luck if they don't seem to respond or want to continue the conversation.

There are many ways of getting around in the Philippines. In addition to the standard boats, buses, trains, taxis, and airlines, there are also uniquely Philippine modes of transport such as pedicabs, kalesa, tricycles, and jeepneys. A kalesa is a horse-drawn carriage; these are often available at historic sites or in very rural areas, such as on farms. Tricycles are motorcycles with attached sidecars. They can carry three to four passengers, so you may have to share the ride with other people. They are best for short trips of a mile or two at most. Pedicabs are like tricycles, except that they are powered by bicycle instead of motorcycle and the attached sidecar can only comfortably sit one passenger. These are good for trips of less than a mile. Jeepneys are modifications of American Jeeps. The shorter type can normally seat twelve to fifteen people, and is good for rides of ten to fifteen miles. The longer, often vibrantly decorated types can seat up to nineteen people and have stereos that blast contemporary music.

Even if you are accustomed to using public transportation at home, you're likely to be surprised by the way it operates in the Philippines. If you are seated near the driver when riding in a jeepney, for example, you will need to pass along the fare, or *pamasahe,* of other passengers seated far from the driver. Note that jeepney drivers have a keen sense of knowing who has and hasn't paid their fare yet.

If you wish to disembark, simply say *para* ("stop"). There may also be a string you can pull that is tied to a lightbulb or bell that will catch the driver's attention. If the driver fails to stop, you can knock loudly on the ceiling of the jeepney—but do this only as a last resort. Don't be surprised if you see people hanging from the rear and sides of jeepneys, or even riding atop them. This is also true to a lesser extent with tricycles. In some rural areas, public transportation passes by infrequently and if you miss it, you may have to wait a while to catch another ride.

Westerners may also be unaccustomed to other aspects of public transportation that are considered normal in some areas in the Philippines. When riding regular buses to the provinces, as in many other countries in Asia, do not be surprised if you see people carrying things such as vegetables, household wares, or even chickens. If you do not care for this sort of thing, try to get on one of the air-conditioned tourist buses, which provide services that are comparable to what you would find in the West. However, such long-distance buses normally accommodate peddlers who sell drinks and snack foods such as peanuts, boiled corn, or bottled water. If you are concerned about sanitation and safety, it's best to bring your own snacks and drinks.

The Philippines is known for its laissez faire traffic situation. While Filipinos are generally courteous and kind, do not expect the same treatment in traffic. Any newcomer would do well to find assistance or advice before even attempting to cross the street. If you plan to walk in the city, do not expect cars to stop for you even when you are using the pedestrian lane. You need to cross the road as you were taught to in grade school—look to your left and right and keep looking until you reach the other side of the street. For safety's sake, make no assumptions on the road.

You can also get around on foot using pedestrian bridges in some urban centers, such as in the Makati financial district of

Metro Manila. Before these bridges, it was uncommon for the working crowd to walk even medium distances around midday because of the heat. But now a lot of people prefer to walk short to long distances instead of wasting time driving in the traffic.

In Manila, which is known for its difficult traffic situation, a long-running traffic rule has helped ease the situation. This number-coding (sometimes also called color-coding) scheme uses the last number of a private vehicle's license plate to determine one day per week that it cannot be on the road. Your Filipino hosts' travel plans may depend on this number coding system.

CHAPTER 28

Doing Business

English is the language of business in the Philippines. Business meetings and transactions are normally conducted in English, and contracts are usually written in it. In many other ways, however, business here is very different from business in the West.

Some foreigners express exasperation over endless inefficiencies encountered while trying to do business in the Philippines. Although this has improved in the past few years because of forward-thinking local government and civic leaders in progressive urban areas, it may still take a while to process local business permits or get things done in remote rural areas.

Unfortunately for those who want to do business here, corruption can also be a concern. Corruption is a phenomenon that happens not only in the Philippines but also in many other countries. It is a problem that has a long history and may take many decades to eradicate, if it can be eradicated at all. To avoid dealing with corruption it is best to be equipped with some knowledge and understanding of the best way to do business locally. Trusted local contacts can advise you about this. It also helps to know that some areas are more impacted by corruption than others.

In the Philippines, as in most Asian countries, it is a good idea to get to know your individual contacts before doing business with them. You can minimize your exposure to corruption by choosing the people you deal with very carefully and knowing them before making any final agreement with them. Some investors or businessmen may decide to go out for lunch, dinner, or to have a few drinks together, so they will feel at ease with each other. Still other businessmen may decide on key issues over a game of golf.

Because corruption might occur while doing business away from the office, progressive politicians and business executives who wish to make a difference and institute change only conduct business in their offices.

If someone asks you for a bribe or kickback from a transaction, explain to him or her in a nonthreatening manner that this goes against your company's policies. For example, if while seeking a business permit you come across someone who seems to delay the process, tell him or her that preventing your business activity from continuing would negatively impact the local economy and potentially cost jobs.

It is best to keep in mind that most Filipinos actually wish to do good and the few who are tempted to seek bribes are often driven to do so by economic problems. Try to dissuade the individual by explaining to him or her that taking bribes will actually hurt more than it can help. If the person is adamant in extorting money from you, it is best to find a higher authority that may be able to address the problem and keep it from continuing. Of course, these situations can be extremely tricky and seeking advice from an honest and competent outsider who is familiar with business in the Philippines is also recommended.

When dealing with Filipino staff, keep in mind that many Filipinos give primary importance to personal friendships. They may prefer dealing with a boss who can also be a good friend rather than one who is strictly professional. Note also that relationships of any kind are ruled by *pakikisama* ("getting along with others"), a value esteemed by many Filipinos. If you are new on the job, it may be worth your time to chat with your staff about their needs and aspirations. Because the heart can be even more important than the head in Philippine business, empathy is also highly appreciated by most Filipinos, whether you are the boss or a co-worker.

Do not be surprised if some of your Filipino workers, particularly the minimum-wage earners, request advance pay, or *bale,* in an emergency or if they are in a tight spot. You should probably grant their request but you may consider taking time to counsel them about the wise use of money. Unlike in America and many other Western nations, Filipino employers (particularly at small companies) may also act as counselors of sorts.

Another significant difference between Western and Filipino business practices is the importance of personal relationships when it comes to getting things done. In countries such as the United States, it is said that there are six degrees of separation between any two individuals; in the Philippines, it is probably more like two or three degrees of separation. If you want to locate someone or get something done, a friend or acquaintance will probably know someone who is in a position to reach that person or to handle the situation. That is why there is a saying in Filipino business that "it is not what you know, but who you know that counts." Unfortunately, this sometimes means that favoritism will win out in what should be above-board selections for jobs or projects.

As in other countries, if you are bidding out a job, gifts will often be sent to you. Most private companies in the Philippines will not allow their management and employees to accept these gifts unless they are worth only a small amount of money—perhaps less than US$20. But in situations where there is a selection of suppliers or contractors, it is best to set a policy of not accepting any form of gift. Some suppliers will take offense if you return their gifts, but those who deal regularly with foreign companies and larger Philippine corporations will understand your decision. Depending on your policies, you may either choose to return the gift or simply tell the giver that it will be donated to a charity selected by the company.

Western businesspeople in the Philippines should also keep in mind that in the islands, age and experience are considered worthy of respect. If you are a young expatriate manager, take note that seniority is important here. If you are managing senior workers, try to do so in such a way that recognizes the wisdom that their seniority accords them and gives them due respect.

The influence of the Filipino family extends even to the business world. Most businesses in the Philippines—including large corporations—are family-owned. Even in the case of publicly traded businesses, founding families will usually control large portions of their company's shares.

Be aware of the tendency of Filipinos to affiliate with organizations or movements. For example, college fraternities are popular here. Your employees who come from similar universities or fraternities may tend to group together. Organizations such as the Lions, Rotary, and Jaycees are popular, but there are also other organizations catering to various interests. People wishing to do business in the Philippines may want to join some of these organizations if they agree with their aims and objectives.

CHAPTER 29

Money and
Financial Transactions

Just like everywhere else in the world, it is wise to be very careful when entering into any transaction involving money in the Philippines. The following are some tips that will help you avoid potential pitfalls.

When handling money, always be aware of other people. Do not flash wads of cash or count money in public. When visiting a crowded mall, hold tightly to your handbag or wallet; some people might take advantage of careless individuals by snatching their bags or picking their pockets. Carry only the cash you expect to spend and memorize the emergency information for your credit cards and relevant identity documents in case these things are stolen. You may also want to write this information down and store it in a safe place.

While credit cards are usually honored in metropolitan areas and urban centers in the provinces, there may be some places where you have no choice but to carry cash. Traveler's checks are normally honored in hotels and bigger restaurants, but you may also exchange them for cash at a bank, major mall, or hotel. Don't carry too much cash with you; store some of your valuables and traveler's checks in your hotel's safety deposit box.

Avoid withdrawing money from ATMs located in dark or isolated places. Always be conscious of your immediate surroundings. If you seem to be having trouble using an ATM, you may be approached by a security guard or other bystanders who offer help. While some people are just plain curious or really do want to be helpful, you never know their motives. Insist on your need for privacy. Even the security guard with seemingly good intentions should not see your personal identification number (PIN).

When you enter into any major transaction, such as buying a house or leasing a condo, you can protect yourself by drafting a contract that will be signed by you and the seller and filed with a notary public office. By doing so, you are essentially putting your contract into public files for later reference if you end up in a court case. Keep a copy of the notarized contract, too.

Another way you can protect yourself is by opening a checking account at one of the local or international banks in the Philippines. Checks that you issue as payment for goods or services confirm your transaction because you can eventually obtain your issued checks from the bank. Checks also help protect sellers from fraud because they can file *estafa*, or "fraud," charges against the issuer should the check fail to liquidate.

An additional safety precaution is to issue crossed checks, which is a common practice in the Philippines. This is done by drawing two parallel diagonal lines on the top left-hand corner on the front of any check, and means that the check can only be deposited directly into the payee's bank account and cannot be cashed. This prevents fraud by allowing direct payments only to the intended individuals or institutions.

When personally lending money to other people, be aware that usury (charging very high interest rates) is frowned upon. Banks offer competitive and fair interest rates on loans but also require many documents and proof of identity from potential borrowers. As in other countries, credit card companies impose very high interest rates.

Many investment opportunities are available in the Philippines. However, it is important that you are in a position to monitor and manage your investments. Start-up enterprises or new ventures usually require a certain amount of physical presence on your part. You cannot expect to leave the country and assume that the accountant or manager you hired will take care of everything. Consult a trusted local friend or professional investment manager for advice on making investments in the Philippines.

CHAPTER 30

Filipino Time

O ne source of frustration for foreigners in the Philippines is the Filipino tendency to arrive late for meetings or gatherings. Such tardiness has come to be known to locals as *Filipino time*. Although event invitations may mention a starting time, the event will often actually start thirty to sixty minutes later in anticipation of late comers.

Sometimes there are valid excuses for lateness, such as city traffic, particularly in Metro Manila, where traffic can become very heavy during peak hours. Therefore, it helps if you avoid scheduling events in certain locations during busy times, particularly if the guests are coming from different parts of the city. The best way to minimize your wait for Filipino contacts is to set your appointment time fifteen to thirty minutes earlier than you really intended to meet, or to stress that they must meet you at a particular time.

Ultimately, Westerners should understand that the Filipino perception of time is simply different from the Western one. Filipinos grew up in a cultural environment where life was enjoyed and not treated as a rat race. This mindset can be traced back to more than three hundred years under Spanish rule.

When it comes to work, however, you should enforce the proper time. There is no reason why Filipinos cannot adjust to reporting at the right time if the need to do so is made clear to them. A common practice is that rank-and-file workers are expected to clock in and out on time, while professional managers are exempt because they are not paid for overtime work. A reception guard may record the comings and goings of managers for reference during performance evaluations.

With the country's integration into the global community, including among other things the advent of the call-center industry, Filipino time is slowly disappearing from the lives of many Filipinos. The twentieth century has brought new opportunities that continue to shape and mold the character of the modern Filipino.

CHAPTER 31

Electronic Etiquette

Information technology gadgets and services such as cell phones, laptops, and e-mail allow people to stay connected and in constant touch with friends, families, colleagues, and acquaintances. However, as in many parts of the world, these gadgets have also caused some problems in the Philippines, particularly when they intrude into the privacy or enjoyment of other people.

However, cell phones can be indispensable in the Philippines. They will sometimes be the best—or only—option for communicating with your host, driver, or local friends. Especially in the provinces, landline telephone service will not always be easily available.

It is very easy to acquire a brand new cell phone in the Philippines. Normally these phones require prepaid minutes (as opposed to monthly subscriber plans, which are also available but generally require a two-year commitment) that can be reloaded through prepaid cards or purchased at many stores. Cell phones are available almost everywhere these days, but it is best to buy them at one of the large malls or an authorized retail shop of a local telecom company. If you do not want to get a new phone, your host may have a spare cell phone you could borrow. You can then buy a new subscriber identity module (SIM) card for the phone, which essentially holds a new phone number that you can use throughout your stay in the Philippines. But as cell phones are quite affordable you should consider getting your own if you will be in the country for any length of time.

Carrying a cell phone requires that you observe the proper etiquette for doing so. When attending a religious service or meeting or watching a movie, it is best to turn off your cell phone or put it in silent mode to avoid distracting others.

One means of communication that is nearly silent and therefore more appropriate for use in public places is SMS, or text messaging. Also known as *texting*, this cell-phone technology is quite popular in the Philippines. It allows you to type short messages using your cell phone's keypad and send them to another cell phone, almost like e-mail. The Philippines is often dubbed "the SMS capital of the world," and more text messages are sent here every year than are sent in much more populous countries, including India.

For many foreigners, text messaging is a relatively new phenomenon, but this service is an inexpensive means of communication used by most Filipinos. When you receive text messages from friends or colleagues it is expected that you will respond either by calling them or by replying with your own text message. Some Filipinos can be sensitive when their text messages are ignored. However, you don't need to bother responding to messages from unknown senders.

Remember that there are scams related to text messaging. It's possible that you will get a text message saying that you have won a cash prize and to claim it, you need to provide personal information, such as your bank account number. Ignore these messages. Should they become intrusive, report them to your service provider.

Many laptop users take advantage of the wireless networks and cozy atmosphere found in many modern coffee shops in the Philippines. Should you choose to do work in a café, always be wary of your belongings. It would be best to bring a fully charged laptop instead of relying on the shop's electrical outlet. You might be charged a small fee for your use of the electricity or you might not find a socket that provides the right voltage. (The standard voltage of electricity used by most businesses and residents in the Philippines is 220 volts, 60/Khz.)

An alternative to lugging a laptop through the streets would be to visit an Internet café to do simple electronic chores such as checking e-mail. Internet cafes offer quite inexpensive Internet sevices and are found in many parts of the country, including the provinces. If you are handling sensitive data, however, having your own computer would be advisable.

If you are managing Filipinos it may be best to intersperse your electronic communication with personal contact to avoid misunderstanding. You may write things in your e-mails that could be misunderstood because of cultural differences.

CHAPTER 32

Saying Good-bye

Paalam translates as "good-bye." However, it is a word that is rarely used in daily conversation—perhaps because it has a somber connotation and Filipinos don't like the concept of parting ways with friends, family, or acquaintances. If they need to part ways at all, Filipinos say "bye," which they have adopted from their Western friends. Close friends and family members often part with a hug, kiss on the cheek, or wave (or all three).

Filipinos can be sentimental and may find it difficult to say good-bye, especially in personal situations. It is common to see whole families sending off a relative at the airport. Some of these good-byes will be tearful ones, especially in the cases of overseas foreign worker (OFW) families. Because the economic situation in the country has led many Filipinos to seek work abroad, a father or mother may be separated from his or her young children for many years. This is just one of the many realities that can make good-byes in the Philippines so heart-wrenching.

On the lighter side, good-byes between new business or personal acquaintances are simple. However, good-byes will often be more elaborate for foreign visitors who have been in the country for a long period of time. It is the habit of Filipinos to hold a send-off party, or *despedida*, or host a special lunch or dinner for colleagues with whom they have become close. Unless there is a very good reason to decline, the departing colleague would do well to accept such an invitation. After all, it is simply meant to honor his or her relationship with the group. The departing colleague may also be showered with gifts or tokens of appreciation from friends and office-mates. It is appropriate to accept these things and thank the givers for their generosity. It is also possible, especially in more formal situations, that guests may offer a toast to their colleague.

When you must leave the Philippines, we hope that you will only have pleasant memories of your stay and of the hospitable people you met.

And as we always say, *Mabuhay*! (Long live!)

Helpful Vocabulary

A

Aguinaldo — Christmas gifts given to children by godparents or older people

Amo — Boss, employer, superior

Ate/Kuya — Elder sister/Elder brother

Awa — Pity, compassion

B

Bagà — Lung

Bahala na — Whatever fate brings

Bakante — Vacant

Bale — Advance pay given at the request of an employee

Balut — Boiled duck fetus, a local delicacy

Barong tagalog — A shirt that is part of the traditional formal dress for Filipino men

Basa — Read

Bathala — A spirit divinity who inhabited nature; worshipped by early Filipinos and some indigenous tribes today

Bayanihan — Community team spirit

Beso — Kiss, peck on the cheek

Bihasà — Expert

Bisita — Visit

Bola — Insincere comment

Bolero/mambobola — Someone who gives insincere compliments

Bunso — The youngest member of the family (sometimes used as an endearment)

C

Camison — Cotton undershirt

D

Dagâ — Rat

Damít — Clothing

Delicadeza—Sense of honor or propriety, a willingness to avoid morally questionable acts or behavior

Demanda — Lawsuit; demand

Despedida—A goodbye party

Despedida de soltera — Lavish party thrown for the bride before her wedding

Doble cara — "Double faced," someone who appears to be nice but has a bad side

Dukhâ — Poor

E

Estafa — Fraud

F

Fiestas — Community celebrations

G

Gamót — Medicine

Gawâ — Work

H

Halo-halo — Popular Philippine dessert

Harana — Traditional method still common in the provinces for courting a girl by singing love songs to her; this is often done while the suitor stands beneath a window in his beloved's home

Hiya — A sense of shame or shyness; hesitation to step outside norms

I

Iglesia Ni Kristo — Literally "Church of Christ," a Philippine religious organization

Ilaw ng tahanan — An expression used to describe mothers in Filipino families, meaning "Light of the home"

Illustrados — Used during the Spanish period to describe affluent and educated Filipinos

Indios — Used during the Spanish period to describe uneducated Filipinos

Insulares — Spaniards born in the Philippines during the Spanish period

J

Jeepney — Mode of public transport originally made from converted American Jeeps

Jusi — Cloth made from banana fibers

K

Ka — Comrade or buddy (used in rural areas)

Kabanatà — Chapter

Káwanggawâ — Charity

Kamusta [ka]? — How are you?

Kalesa — Horse-drawn carriage

Kanô — American

Kumpare/Kumare — Term by which godfathers and godmothers address each other; also a modern term of endearment for a friend or an acquaintance

Kuya /Ate — Elder brother/Elder sister

L

Labada — Laundry

Langgám — Ant

Langka — Jackfruit

Lindól — Earthquake

Leche Flan — Custard dessert

Lechon — Roast pig

Lolo/Lola — Grandfather/grandmother

Luhà — Tear

M

Mabuhay! — Customary greeting meaning "long live!"

Mabilís — "fast"; one of the six categories of Filipino words; written with an acute accent mark (´)

Maís — Corn

Magkáisá — Unite

Malumay — One of the six categories of Filipino words

Malumì — One of the six categories of Filipino words; indicated with a grave accent mark (`) on its last letter

Mambobola/Bolero — Someone who is fond of making insincere comments

Mámamayán — Citizen

Mámayâ — Later

Mano—A gesture of respect and request for blessing; a younger person touches the extended hand of an older person (palm facing inward) to his or her forehead, with or without saying *Mano po* ("Please bless me")

Maragsâ — One of the six categories of Filipino words; indicated with a circumflex mark (^)

Maria Clara — Traditional female dress, named after a character in Jose Rizal's novel *Noli Mi Tangere*

Mariín — One of the six categories of Filipino words

Materyales — Materials

Mayabang — Boastful

Mayaman — Rich

Misa de Gallo — Midnight mass that marks the beginning of Christmas Day for Catholics

Mestizos/Mestizas — Multiracial Filipinos, generally used to refer to those with Western blood

N

Nanay/Tatay — Mom/Dad

Nata de coco — Coconut-based delicacy

Ninong/Ninang — Godfather/Godmother

Noche Buena — Catholic feast or celebration on Christmas Eve

O

Opo —Respectful form of *yes*

P

Paalam — Good-bye

Pabasa — Catholic biblical readings during Lent

Pagtanim ng galit — Harboring deep-seated anger

Pakikisama — Conforming to the norms of the group; to get along with others

Paksiw na lechon — Day-old roasted pig cooked in liver sauce

Pámahalaán — Government

Pamahiin — Superstition

Pamanhikan — Tradition of a groom bringing his family to meet his bride's family

Panata — Promise

Paninilbihan — Service done by a suitor for the family of his beloved

Panuelo — Wrap worn by women over their *terno*

Para — "Stop"; a word used when a passenger wants to get off a public transport vehicle

Pasalubong — Gift brought home from a trip

Pasensiya — Patience

Pasensiya ka na — "Please have patience"; a Filipino way of saying "I am sorry"

Pedicab — Bicycle with sidecar that is used to transport one or two passengers

Peninsulares — Term for Spanish residents of the Philippines used during the Spanish period

Penoy — A variant of the *balut* duck egg that contains a less developed fetus

Piña — Cloth made from pineapple fiber

Pinsan — Cousin

Pitakà — Purse

Po — Polite or respect word that can be used like *sir* or *ma'am*; can be used when speaking to both men and women

Pritchon — Fried dish made from leftovers of roasted pig

S

Saya — Traditional skirt

Simbang Gabi — Catholic custom of attending morning mass on the days leading up to Christmas

Sinigang — Sour soup made with vegetables and tamarind or lime, as well as fish, chicken, pork, or seafood

T

Tagay — A shot of alcohol
Tatay/Nanay — Dad/Mom
Tawad na presyo — Bargain price
Telenovelas — long-running television series
Terno — Traditional formal wear for Filipino women
Tiangge — Flea market
Tinola — Chicken and vegetable soup
Tito/Tita — Uncle/Aunt
Tricycle — Motorcycle with sidecar

U

Ube — Yam or yam dessert
Uliran — Exemplary
Ulirang ina — exemplary or model mom
Under the *Saya* — "Under the Skirt'" refers to a henpecked husband
Utang na Loob —To remember favors or acts of kindness and feel beholden to the person who granted them until they have been repaid

V

Visita Iglesia — Catholic tradition of visiting seven churches on Holy Thursday

Y

Yaya — Nanny

Index